THE 30-MINUTE
MEDITERRANEAN DIET
AIR FRYER COOKBOOK
FOR BEGINNERS:

150 Quick, Easy, and Delicious Recipes to Boost Your
Healthy Lifestyle. 30-Day Meal Plan Included

James Marcelli

Table of Contents

Welcome to Your New Culinary Adventure!

Welcome to a culinary adventure that blends the vibrant flavors of the Mediterranean with the convenience and efficiency of air frying. In "The 30-Minute Mediterranean Air Fryer Cookbook for Beginners," you'll discover a world where healthy eating meets simplicity, making it easier than ever to enjoy delicious, nutritious meals even on the busiest of days.

Imagine the sun-drenched landscapes of Greece, Italy, and Spain, where meals are a celebration of fresh, wholesome ingredients and family gatherings. With each recipe, you'll be transported to these Mediterranean shores, savoring dishes that are not only good for your body but also for your soul.

Whether you're a seasoned cook or a kitchen novice, this cookbook is your guide to mastering the art of Mediterranean cooking with an air fryer. Embrace the ease of preparation, the speed of cooking, and the delightful flavors that await you.

As you embark on this journey, remember that cooking is not just about following recipes; it's about exploring new tastes, creating memories, and nourishing yourself and your loved ones. Let this book be your companion in the kitchen, inspiring you to create meals that are as delightful to prepare as they are to eat.

Welcome to a healthier, more flavorful way of cooking. Let's get started!

With gratitude,
James Marcelli, your culinary companion

If you'd like to share a brief review, simply scan the QR code. Your honest feedback is invaluable.

Introduction

Hello, fellow food enthusiasts! I'm delighted that you've chosen to embark on this exciting culinary journey with "The 30-Minute Mediterranean Diet Air Fryer Cookbook for Beginners." Whether you are looking to transform your eating habits, delve into the delights of Mediterranean cuisine, or add a spark of innovation to your daily meals, this cookbook is your gateway to a world of flavorful, healthy, and remarkably simple dishes – all made possible with the help of your air fryer.

This cookbook was crafted with a singular vision: to combine the age-old wisdom of Mediterranean eating with the modern convenience of air fryer technology. The Mediterranean diet is celebrated globally for its vibrant flavors and health benefits, ranging from enhanced heart health to longevity. However, embracing this lifestyle can seem daunting, especially if you're juggling a busy schedule. That's where your air fryer comes in. By integrating these two elements, this cookbook aims to show you how to prepare quick, nutritious meals without sacrificing taste or quality.

Key Principles of the Mediterranean Diet

Nutritionists and health professionals worldwide laud the Mediterranean diet for its balanced approach to eating. Here are some of its fundamental principles:

1. **Plant-Based Predominance**: The diet emphasizes a high intake of vegetables, fruits, whole grains, and legumes. These form the base of every meal, providing essential vitamins, minerals, fibers, and antioxidants.

2. **Healthy Fats**: Olive oil is the primary source of fat, used generously to cook and dress dishes. Rich in monounsaturated fats and antioxidants, it replaces less healthy fats and is central to the diet's heart-healthy reputation.

3. **Moderate Protein Consumption**: Fish and seafood are eaten regularly, providing high-quality protein and omega-3 fatty acids. Poultry, eggs, cheese, and yogurt are also consumed in moderation, while red meats are enjoyed on a less frequent basis.

4. **Herbs and Spices**: Instead of salt, meals are flavored with a variety of herbs and spices, which reduces sodium intake and adds unique flavors.

5. **Limited Processed Foods**: The diet avoids heavily processed foods and sweets, focusing instead on food in its most natural form.

6. **Wine in Moderation**: For those who consume alcohol, wine is enjoyed in moderation, usually with meals, contributing to the dietary pattern's cardiovascular benefits.

Scientific Support for the Mediterranean Diet

Numerous studies have shown that the Mediterranean diet can lead to significant health improvements. Key research findings include:

- **Cardiovascular Health**: One of the most well-documented benefits of the Mediterranean diet is its positive impact on heart health. Research indicates that this diet can reduce the risk of developing cardiovascular diseases, including heart attacks and strokes. This is largely due to the diet's emphasis on heart-healthy fats found in olive oil, nuts, and fish, which help lower bad cholesterol levels and increase good cholesterol.

- **Weight Management**: The Mediterranean diet is also beneficial for maintaining a healthy weight. High in fiber and rich in whole foods, it promotes satiety and helps regulate appetite. Unlike restrictive diets, it offers a sustainable approach to weight loss that can be maintained over a lifetime without sacrificing the enjoyment of food.

- **Longevity and Preventing Chronic Diseases**: Adherence to the Mediterranean diet has been associated with increased life expectancy and a lower incidence of chronic diseases, particularly those related to inflammation and oxidative stress, such as type 2 diabetes and certain types of cancer. The antioxidants found in fruits, vegetables, and olive oil play a crucial role in protecting the body from cellular damage.

Guide to Using an Air Fryer

Welcome to the world of air frying, where convenience meets health and deliciousness. Whether you're a seasoned chef or a kitchen novice, this guide is designed to introduce you to the basics of air frying, from understanding how your appliance works to mastering the art of cooking delicious meals with minimal effort and maximum flavor.

How Air Fryers Work

An air fryer operates using a combination of rapid air technology and a top-mounted heating element. Air is heated and then circulated at high speed by a powerful fan, creating a convection effect. This method cooks the food evenly and quickly from all sides, mimicking the crispy finish that traditional frying offers but without the need for submerging the food in oil.

Benefits of Cooking with an Air Fryer

- **Healthier Meals:** Air fryers dramatically decrease the amount of oil needed, cutting fat and calories in dishes. Cooking at lower temperatures for shorter durations helps maintain nutrients, especially in vegetables and proteins.

- **Quick and Efficient:** Air fryers cook food faster than traditional ovens, perfect for fast and healthy meals.

- **Safe and User-Friendly:** Features like automatic shut-off and cool-touch exteriors make air fryers safe and easy to operate.

- **Energy Efficient**: Uses less energy and emits less heat, making air fryers an eco-friendly kitchen appliance.

- **Easy Cleanup:** Air fryers have non-stick surfaces and dishwasher-safe parts, simplifying the cleaning process after cooking.

Practical Tips for Efficiently Using an Air Fryer in Mediterranean Cooking

Maximize your air fryer's potential with these streamlined tips, tailored for the vibrant and healthful Mediterranean cuisine:

- **Versatile Cooking**: Perfectly roast vegetables like bell peppers and zucchinis with a sprinkle of herbs and a drizzle of olive oil. For proteins like fish and poultry, enhance with Mediterranean herbs such as rosemary and thyme to achieve a juicy interior and crispy exterior.

- **Crispy Snacks**: Utilize the air fryer for legumes and grains to create crispy textures; make snacks like chickpeas or falafel quickly and easily.

- **Baked Goods and Flatbreads**: Efficiently bake desserts and reheat or toast flatbreads to complement dips such as hummus or baba ghanoush, achieving a delightful crunch.

- **Using Oil**: A light spray or brushing of oil on foods, especially vegetables, helps achieve an even golden color and improves texture.

- **Cooking in Batches**: Avoid overcrowding by cooking in batches, ensuring even cooking and perfect results every time.

- **Using Accessories**: Enhance your cooking with accessories such as parchment liners or specific air fryer pans to prevent sticking, which is particularly useful for delicate items or baking tasks.

Basic Operation

1. Preheating:

- Most air fryers benefit from preheating, which can take anywhere from 1-5 minutes, depending on the model. This ensures your food cooks evenly.

2. Cooking:

- **Filling the Basket**: Avoid overcrowding the basket to allow hot air to circulate freely. This ensures all pieces cook evenly and get that desired crispiness.
- **Shaking or Flipping**: For most foods, it's beneficial to shake the basket or flip the items halfway through cooking to promote even browning and crispiness.

3. Timing and Temperature:

- Cooking times can vary significantly from traditional methods. Use the guidebook that comes with your air fryer as a starting point and adjust based on your observations.
- Temperature control is crucial. Most air fryers cook effectively between 350°F and 400°F.

Advanced Techniques

- **Baking**: Try cakes, muffins, or even bread.
- **Dehydrating**: Some models come with this functionality, perfect for making dried fruits or jerky.
- **Reheating**: Air fryers are great for reviving leftovers, returning them to their original crispness and warmth.

Essential Ingredients for Mediterranean Cuisine

The foundation of Mediterranean cuisine is built on a variety of fresh and wholesome ingredients that are not only flavorful but also packed with nutrients. Here are some of the key staples:

- **Olive Oil**: The cornerstone of Mediterranean cooking, used for cooking, dressing salads, and as a dip.
- **Fresh Vegetables and Fruits**: Such as tomatoes, bell peppers, zucchinis, eggplants, and leafy greens, which are used abundantly. Citrus fruits, figs, and grapes, which are often used to add natural sweetness or a tangy flavor to dishes.
- **Herbs and Spices**: Including basil, oregano, rosemary, thyme, and saffron, which are essential for adding depth and aroma.

- **Proteins**: Fish and seafood are prevalent along the coast, while legumes like lentils and chickpeas are common in daily meals.

- **Nuts and Seeds**: Such as almonds, pistachios, and sesame seeds, which are often used in salads, desserts, or as snacks.

- **Whole Grains**: Like barley, bulgur, and farro, which form the base for many nutritious dishes.

- **Cheeses and Yogurt**: Feta, halloumi, and Greek yogurt are dairy staples, adding creaminess and a tangy flavor to meals.

- **Bread and Pasta**: Integral parts of meals, often homemade or selected for freshness.

APPETIZERS

AIR-FRIED FALAFEL

SERVES 4 | PREP 15 MIN | COOK 20 MIN

INGREDIENTS

1 cup dried chickpeas, soaked overnight

1 small onion, chopped

3 cloves garlic, minced

1/4 cup fresh parsley, chopped

2 Tbsp fresh cilantro, chopped

1 tsp ground cumin

1 tsp ground coriander

1/2 tsp salt

1/4 tsp black pepper

1/4 tsp cayenne pepper

1 tsp lemon juice

2 Tbsp all-purpose flour

1 tsp baking powder

Olive oil spray

DIRECTIONS

- Drain and rinse the soaked chickpeas.
- In a food processor, combine chickpeas, onion, garlic, parsley, cilantro, cumin, coriander, salt, black pepper, cayenne pepper, and lemon juice. Process until mixture is finely ground.
- Transfer to a bowl, and stir in flour and baking powder.
- Form the mixture into small balls, about 1.5 inches in diameter.
- Preheat the air fryer to 375°F (190°C).
- Place falafel balls in the air fryer basket. Spray lightly with olive oil.
- Cook for 10 minutes, turn the falafel over, spray again, and cook for an additional 10 minutes or until golden and crispy.

Per serving (approximately 4 falafels): calories 265; fat 6g; protein 9g; carbs 45g; fiber 8g

BRUSCHETTA WITH TOMATO AND BASIL

SERVES 4 | PREP 10 MIN | COOK 5 MIN

INGREDIENTS

4 large ripe tomatoes, finely chopped

1/4 cup fresh basil leaves, chopped

2 cloves garlic, minced

1 Tbsp balsamic vinegar

2 Tbsp olive oil, plus extra for brushing

1/2 tsp salt

1/4 tsp black pepper

1 baguette, sliced into 1/2-inch-thick slices

DIRECTIONS

- Combine the chopped tomatoes, basil, garlic, balsamic vinegar, 2 tablespoons of olive oil, salt, and pepper in a bowl. Stir together until well mixed.
- Brush each slice of baguette lightly with olive oil on both sides.
- Toast the baguette slices in the air fryer at 350°F (175°C) for about 5 minutes, or until they are golden and crispy.
- Top each toasted bread slice generously with the tomato mixture. Serve immediately.

Per serving (approximately 3 slices): calories 215; fat 7g; protein 6g; carbs 32g; fiber 2g

SPANAKOPITA TRIANGLES

SERVES 4 | PREP 20 MIN | COOK 15 MIN

INGREDIENTS

1/2 lb spinach, fresh

1/2 cup feta cheese, crumbled

1/4 cup ricotta cheese

1 small onion, finely chopped

2 cloves garlic, minced

1 Tbsp dill, chopped

1 Tbsp parsley, chopped

1/4 tsp salt

1/4 tsp black pepper

1 egg, beaten

10 sheets phyllo dough, thawed

Olive oil spray

DIRECTIONS

- Sauté onion and garlic in olive oil until soft, then add spinach and cook until wilted. Let cool.
- Mix the spinach with feta, ricotta, egg, dill, salt, and pepper.
- Preheat the air fryer to 375°F (190°C).
- Cut phyllo into 3-inch-wide strips, cover unused phyllo with a damp cloth.
- Place a tablespoon of filling at one end of a strip, fold into a triangle, continuing like a flag.
- Brush triangles with butter or oil, place in the air fryer without overcrowding.
- Cook for 15 minutes or until golden.
- Serve immediately.

Per serving (approximately 3 triangles): calories 190; fat 9g; protein 9g; carbs 18g; fiber 2g

CRISPY ARTICHOKE HEARTS

SERVES 4 | PREP 10 MIN | COOK 8 MIN

INGREDIENTS

1 can (14 oz) artichoke hearts, drained and quartered

1/4 cup all-purpose flour

1/2 tsp garlic powder

1/2 tsp onion powder

1/4 tsp salt

1/4 tsp black pepper

2 eggs, beaten

1 cup panko breadcrumb

Olive oil spray

DIRECTIONS

- Pat the artichoke hearts dry with paper towels to remove excess moisture.
- In a small bowl, mix flour, garlic powder, onion powder, salt, and pepper.
- Dip each artichoke heart into the flour mixture, then into the beaten eggs, and finally coat with panko breadcrumbs.
- Preheat the air fryer to 375°F (190°C).
- Arrange the breaded artichoke hearts in the air fryer basket in a single layer. Spray lightly with olive oil.
- Cook for 7-8 minutes; flip the artichoke hearts, spray again with olive oil, and cook for another 7-8 minutes or until golden and crispy. Serve immediately.

Per serving (approximately 6 pieces): calories 180; fat 5g; protein 7g; carbs 28g; fiber 3g

MEDITERRANEAN STUFFED PEPPERS

SERVES 4 | PREP 15 MIN | COOK 20 MIN

INGREDIENTS

4 bell peppers, tops cut off and
seeded
1 cup cooked quinoa
1/2 cup feta cheese, crumbled
1/4 cup black olives, chopped
1/4 cup red onion, finely chopped
1/4 cup fresh parsley, chopped
2 Tbsp olive oil
1 tsp garlic powder
1/2 tsp salt
1/4 tsp black pepper

DIRECTIONS

- Preheat the air fryer to 360°F (182°C).
- In a bowl, combine quinoa, feta cheese, black olives, red onion, parsley, olive oil, garlic powder, salt, and pepper.
- Stuff the mixture into the hollowed peppers.
- Place the stuffed peppers in the air fryer basket.
- Cook for 15-20 minutes or until the peppers are tender and the filling is heated through.

Per serving (1 stuffed pepper): calories 220; fat 11g; protein 6g; carbs 27g; fiber 5g

ZUCCHINI CHIPS

SERVES 4 | PREP 10 MIN | COOK 10 MIN

INGREDIENTS

2 large zucchinis, thinly sliced
1 Tbsp olive oil
1/2 tsp salt
1/4 tsp black pepper
1/2 tsp paprika

DIRECTIONS

- Toss zucchini slices in olive oil, salt, pepper, and paprika.
- Preheat the air fryer to 375°F (190°C).
- Arrange zucchini slices in a single layer in the air fryer basket.
- Cook for 5 minutes, flip the slices, and cook for another 5 minutes or until crispy.

Per serving (1/4 of total): calories 60; fat 4g; protein 2g; carbs 6g; fiber 2g

KALE CHIPS

INGREDIENTS

1 bunch kale, washed, dried, and torn into bite-size pieces

1 Tbsp olive oil

1/2 tsp salt

DIRECTIONS

- Toss kale pieces with olive oil and salt.
- Preheat the air fryer to 360°F (182°C).
- Place kale in the air fryer basket in a single layer.
- Cook for 2 minutes, shake the basket, and cook for another 2-3 minutes or until crispy.

Per serving: calories 58; fat 4g; protein 2g; carbs 5g; fiber 1g

FETA CHEESE BITES

INGREDIENTS

1 cup feta cheese, cut into 1/2-inch cubes

1/2 cup all-purpose flour

1 egg, beaten

1 cup panko breadcrumbs

Olive oil spray

DIRECTIONS

- Coat feta cubes first in flour, then dip in beaten egg, and finally coat with panko breadcrumbs.
- Preheat the air fryer to 350°F (177°C).
- Place feta bites in the air fryer basket, spray lightly with olive oil.
- Cook for 5 minutes or until golden and crispy.

Per serving (1/4 of total): calories 198; fat 12g; protein 9g; carbs 15g; fiber 1g

AIR-FRIED OLIVES

SERVES 4 | PREP 10 MIN | COOK 10 MIN

INGREDIENTS

1 cup green olives, pitted

1/2 cup flour

1 egg, beaten

1 cup panko breadcrumb

Olive oil spray

DIRECTIONS

- Coat olives in flour, dip in beaten egg, then coat with panko breadcrumbs.
- Preheat the air fryer to 360°F (182°C).
- Place olives in the air fryer basket, spray with olive oil.
- Cook for 5 minutes, shake the basket, and cook for another 5 minutes until crispy.

Per serving (1/4 of total): calories 210; fat 15g; protein

BABA GHANOUSH WITH AIR-FRIED VEGGIE CHIPS

SERVES 4 | PREP 15 MIN | COOK 20 MIN

INGREDIENTS

For the baba ghanoush:

1 large eggplant, halved lengthwise

3 Tbsp tahini

2 cloves garlic, minced

2 Tbsp lemon juice

1/4 tsp salt

1/4 tsp cumin

2 Tbsp olive oil

For the veggie chips:

2 carrots, thinly sliced

1 zucchini, thinly sliced

Olive oil spray

1/2 tsp salt

DIRECTIONS

- For the baba ghanoush, roast eggplant in the air fryer at 400°F (204°C) for 20 minutes. Scoop out the flesh and blend with tahini, garlic, lemon juice, salt, cumin, and olive oil until smooth.
- For the veggie chips, spray carrot and zucchini slices with olive oil and sprinkle with salt.
- Preheat the air fryer to 375°F (190°C).
- Cook veggie chips for 10 minutes, shake the basket, and cook for another 10 minutes until crispy.
- Serve baba ghanoush with veggie chips.

Per serving: calories 220; fat 15g; protein 4g; carbs 20g; fiber 6g

GARLIC SHRIMPS

INGREDIENTS

1 lb shrimp, peeled and deveined

3 cloves garlic, minced

2 Tbsp olive oil

1/2 tsp paprika

1/4 tsp salt

1/4 tsp black pepper

1 Tbsp lemon juice

DIRECTIONS

- In a bowl, mix shrimp, garlic, olive oil, paprika, salt, pepper, and lemon juice.
- Preheat the air fryer to 400°F (204°C).
- Place shrimp in the air fryer basket in a single layer.
- Cook for 4 minutes, flip the shrimp, and cook for another 4 minutes or until cooked through.

Per serving (1/4 of total): calories 174; fat 8g; protein 23g; carbs 2g; fiber 0g

MOZZARELLA STICKS

SERVES 4 | PREP 10 MIN | COOK 6 MIN

INGREDIENTS

8 mozzarella cheese sticks, halved

1/2 cup all-purpose flour

1 egg, beaten

1 cup panko breadcrumb

1/2 tsp Italian seasoning

Olive oil spray

DIRECTIONS

- Freeze mozzarella sticks for at least an hour.
- Coat in flour, dip in beaten egg, then coat with a mixture of panko breadcrumbs and Italian seasoning.
- Preheat the air fryer to 400°F (204°C).
- Place mozzarella sticks in the air fryer basket, spray with olive oil.
- Cook for 3 minutes, flip, and cook for another 3 minutes or until golden and crispy.

Per serving (4 pieces): calories 270; fat 15g; protein 15g; carbs 18g; fiber 1g

HUMMUS PLATE WITH AIR-FRIED PITA CHIPS

SERVES 4 | PREP 10 MIN | COOK 8 MIN

INGREDIENTS

For the hummus:
1 can (15 oz) chickpeas, drained and rinsed
1/4 cup tahini
2 cloves garlic, minced
2 Tbsp olive oil
2 Tbsp lemon juice
1/2 tsp salt

For the pita chips:
4 pita bread rounds, cut into eighths
Olive oil spray
1/2 tsp salt.

DIRECTIONS

- For the hummus, blend all ingredients in a food processor until smooth.
- For the pita chips, spray pita pieces with olive oil and sprinkle with salt.
- Preheat the air fryer to 360°F (182°C).
- Place pita chips in the air fryer basket. Cook for 4 minutes, shake the basket, and cook for another 4 minutes until crispy.
- Serve hummus with pita chips.

Per serving: calories 348; fat 18g; protein 9g; carbs 40g; fiber 7g

GREEK MEATBALLS

SERVES 4 | PREP 15 MIN | COOK 12 MIN

INGREDIENTS

1 lb ground lamb or beef

1/4 cup breadcrumbs

1 egg

1/4 cup onion, finely chopped

2 cloves garlic, minced

1 Tbsp fresh mint, chopped

1 Tbsp fresh parsley, chopped

1/2 tsp salt

1/4 tsp black pepper

1/2 tsp cumin.

DIRECTIONS

- In a bowl, mix all ingredients until well combined.
- Form mixture into 1-inch meatballs.
- Preheat the air fryer to 400°F (204°C).
- Place meatballs in the air fryer basket in a single layer.
- Cook for 6 minutes, turn the meatballs, and cook for another 6 minutes or until fully cooked.

Per serving (approximately 4 meatballs): calories 295; fat 20g; protein 22g; carbs 5g; fiber 1g

HALLOUMI FRIES

SERVES 4 | PREP 10 MIN | COOK 8 MIN

INGREDIENTS

8 oz halloumi cheese, cut into fries

1/4 cup flour

1 tsp paprika

Olive oil spray

DIRECTIONS

- Toss halloumi fries with flour and paprika.
- Preheat the air fryer to 400°F (204°C).
- Place halloumi fries in the air fryer basket and spray with olive oil.
- Cook for 4 minutes. Flip the fries, spray again, and cook for another 4 minutes until crispy and golden.

Per serving: calories 250; fat 18g; protein 16g; carbs 9g; fiber 0g

CRISPY CAULIFLOWER WITH TAHINI SAUCE

SERVES 4 | PREP 15 MIN | COOK 20 MIN

INGREDIENTS

1 head cauliflower, cut into florets

1 cup flour

1/2 tsp salt

1/2 tsp pepper

1 tsp garlic powder

2 eggs, beaten

1 cup panko breadcrumb

For the tahini sauce:

1/4 cup tahini

2 Tbsp lemon juice

1 clove garlic, minced

1/4 tsp salt

DIRECTIONS

- Coat cauliflower florets in flour mixed with salt, pepper, and garlic powder. Dip in eggs, then coat in breadcrumbs.
- Preheat the air fryer to 400°F (204°C).
- Cook florets for 10 minutes, shake the basket, and cook for another 10 minutes until crispy.
- For the sauce, whisk tahini, lemon juice, garlic, and salt. Add water until the desired consistency is reached.
- Serve cauliflower with tahini sauce drizzled over or on the side.

Per serving: calories 280; fat 14g; protein 10g; carbs 32g; fiber 5g

EGGPLANT ROLLATINI

INGREDIENTS

1 large eggplant, sliced lengthwise (1/4 inch thick)

1 cup ricotta cheese

1/4 cup grated Parmesan

1 egg

2 Tbsp chopped basil

1 cup marinara sauce

1/2 cup shredded mozzarella

DIRECTIONS

- Sprinkle eggplant slices with salt, sit for 10 minutes, then pat dry.
- Mix ricotta, Parmesan, egg, and basil in a bowl.
- Spread each eggplant slice with the cheese mixture, roll it up, and secure it with a toothpick.
- Spread a thin layer of marinara in an air fryer-safe dish. Place rolls seam side down. Top with remaining sauce and mozzarella.
- Cook at 360°F (182°C) for 15 minutes or until cheese is bubbly and browned.

Per serving: calories 220; fat 12g; protein 14g; carbs 15g;

MUSHROOM CAPS WITH HERB CHEESE

INGREDIENTS

12 large mushroom caps, stems removed

1 cup cream cheese, softened

2 Tbsp fresh herbs (chives, parsley, thyme), chopped

DIRECTIONS

- Mix cream cheese, herbs, and garlic.
- Stuff each mushroom cap with the cheese mixture.
- Spray lightly with olive oil.
- Cook in the air fryer at 350°F (177°C) for 10 minutes or until mushrooms are tender and filling is heated through

Per serving: calories 150; fat 12g; protein 4g; carbs 6g; fiber 1g

AIR-FRIED COD CAKES

SERVES 4 | PREP 20 MIN | COOK 6 MIN

INGREDIENTS

1 lb cod fillets, cooked and flaked

1 cup mashed potatoes

1 egg, beaten

2 Tbsp chopped parsley

1 tsp lemon zest

1/2 tsp salt

1/4 tsp pepper

1 cup panko breadcrumbs

Olive oil spray

DIRECTIONS

- Mix cod, potatoes, egg, parsley, lemon zest, salt, and pepper. Form into patties. Coat in breadcrumbs.
- Spray with olive oil.
- Cook in the air fryer at 390°F (200°C) for 3 minutes, flip, spray again, and cook for another 3 minutes until golden.

Per serving: calories 240; fat 4g; protein 21g; carbs 30g; fiber 2g; sodium 350mg

LEMON HERB SCALLOPS

SERVES 4 | PREP 10 MIN | COOK 6 MIN

INGREDIENTS

12 large scallops

2 Tbsp olive oil

1 Tbsp lemon juice

1 tsp chopped herbs (parsley, thyme)

1/4 tsp salt

1/4 tsp pepper

DIRECTIONS

- Toss scallops with olive oil, lemon juice, herbs, salt, and pepper.
- Cook in the air fryer at 390°F (204°C) for 3 minutes, flip, and cook for another 3 minutes until opaque and slightly firm

Per serving: calories 110; fat 5g; protein 14g; carbs 2g; fiber 0g; sodium 220mg

FISH & SEAFOOD

Tips from the Author

"Experiment with cooking times and temperatures to perfect your air fryer fish dishes. Thinner fillets may need less time, while thicker cuts might require a few extra minutes. With a bit of practice, you'll master the perfect balance for delicious, healthy seafood."

PISTACHIO CRUSTED SALMON

INGREDIENTS

2 salmon fillets (6 oz each)

1/4 cup chopped pistachios

1 Tbsp Dijon mustard

1 Tbsp honey

½ tsp garlic powder

Salt and pepper, to taste

Olive oil spray

DIRECTIONS

- Pat dry the salmon with paper towels.
- Sprinkle salt, pepper, and garlic powder.
- Using a spoon or a brush, spread the Dijon mustard over the fillets first, then layer with honey.
- Finely chop pistachios and spread them evenly on top, pressing into the salmon to ensure they stick.
- Preheat the air fryer to 400°F (204°C). Spray the basket with oil spray.
- Place the fillets in the air-fryer basket, pistachio-side up, and cook for about 8-10 minutes until the salmon is cooked through and the crust is golden.

Per serving (1 fillet): calories 320; fat 15g; protein 34g; carbs 12g; fiber 2g.

GARLIC BUTTER SHRIMP

INGREDIENTS

1 lb shrimp, peeled and deveined

3 Tbsp butter, melted

3 cloves garlic, minced

1 Tbsp lemon juice

1 Tbsp fresh parsley, chopped

Salt and pepper to taste

DIRECTIONS

- Mix butter with spices and lemon juice in a bowl.
- Add the shrimp and mix well.
- Arrange the air fryer in a single layer.
- Air fryer at 400°F (204°C) for 6-8 minutes, shaking the basket halfway.

Per serving: calories 210; fat 12g; protein 24g; carbs 1g; fiber 0g

MEDITERRANEAN TUNA PATTIES

SERVES 4 | PREP 15 MIN | COOK 10 MIN

INGREDIENTS

2 cans (5 oz each) tuna in olive oil, drained

1/2 cup breadcrumbs

1/4 cup Kalamata olives, finely chopped

1/4 cup sun-dried tomatoes, finely chopped

1/4 cup feta cheese, crumbled

2 tablespoons fresh parsley, chopped

1 egg, beaten

1 clove garlic, minced

1 lemon, zested

Salt and pepper, to taste

Olive oil spray

DIRECTIONS

- Combine the tuna, breadcrumbs, olives, sun-dried tomatoes, feta cheese, parsley, egg, garlic, and lemon zest in a large bowl. Season with salt and pepper.
- Mix everything together until well combined. If the mixture is too dry, add olive oil or water to moisten.
- Shape the mixture into 8 patties.
- Preheat the air fryer to 375°F (190°C). Spray the air fryer basket with olive oil spray.
- Place the patties in the basket, making sure they do not touch. Spray the tops of the patties lightly with olive oil.
- Cook for 5 minutes. Flip the patties and spray the other side lightly with olive oil. Cook for an additional 5 minutes or until golden and firm.
- Serve the patties warm, with a side of mixed greens or sauce.

Per serving: calories 210; fat 8g; protein 22g; carbs 12g; fiber 2g

LEMON DILL SALMON

SERVES 4 | PREP 5 MIN | COOK 8-10 MIN

INGREDIENTS

4 salmon fillets (6 oz each)

2 Tbsp olive oil

1 Tbsp fresh dill, chopped

2 lemons, one juiced and one sliced

Salt and pepper to taste

DIRECTIONS

- Mix olive oil, lemon juice, dill, salt, and pepper.
- Brush mixture over salmon fillets.
- Top each fillet with lemon slices.
- Cook in the air fryer at 400°F (204°C) for 8-10 minutes.

Per serving: calories 330; fat 20g; protein 34g; carbs 3g; fiber 1g

SALMON WITH PESTO SAUCE

SERVES 4 | PREP 5 MIN | COOK 8-10 MIN

INGREDIENTS

- 4 salmon fillets (6 oz each)
- 4 Tbsp pesto
- 1 lemon, sliced
- Salt and pepper to taste

DIRECTIONS

- Season salmon with salt and pepper.
- Spread 1 Tbsp of pesto on top of each fillet.
- Top with lemon slices.
- Cook in the air fryer at 400°F (204°C) for 8-10 minutes.

Per serving: calories 340; fat 22g; protein 34g; carbs 2g; fiber 0g

CRISPY AIR-FRIED CALAMARI

SERVES 4 | PREP 15 MIN | COOK 6 MIN

INGREDIENTS

- 1 lb calamari, cleaned and cut into rings
- 1 cup all-purpose flour
- 1/2 tsp salt
- 1/2 tsp black pepper
- 1 tsp paprika
- 2 eggs, beaten
- 1 cup panko breadcrumbs
- Olive oil spray

DIRECTIONS

- In a bowl, combine flour, salt, pepper, and paprika.
- Place beaten eggs in a separate bowl and panko breadcrumbs in another bowl.
- Dip each calamari ring into the flour mixture, then the beaten eggs, and finally coat with panko breadcrumbs.
- Preheat the air fryer to 375°F (190°C). Spray the air fryer basket with olive oil spray.
- Arrange the calamari rings in a single layer in the basket, ensuring they do not overlap. Spray the calamari lightly with olive oil.
- Cook for 3 minutes, flip the calamari rings, spray again, and cook for another 3 minutes or until golden and crispy.
- Serve immediately with lemon wedges and your choice of dipping sauce.

Per serving: calories 250; fat 5g; protein 18g; carbs 30g; fiber 2g

MEDITERRANEAN SALMON STEAK

INGREDIENTS

4 salmon steaks (about 6 oz each)

2 Tbsp olive oil

1 lemon, sliced

1/4 cup Kalamata olives, pitted and halved

1/4 cup sun-dried tomatoes, chopped

2 cloves garlic, minced

1 tsp dried oregano

Salt and pepper, to taste

Fresh parsley, chopped (for garnish

DIRECTIONS

- In a small bowl, combine olive oil, garlic, oregano, salt, and pepper.
- Brush the olive oil mixture over both sides of the salmon steaks.
- Arrange lemon slices on top of each steak.
- Preheat the air fryer to 400°F (204°C).
- Place the salmon steaks in the air fryer basket. Scatter Kalamata olives and sun-dried tomatoes around the salmon.
- Cook for 8-10 minutes until the salmon is cooked through and flakes easily with a fork.
- Garnish with fresh parsley before serving.

Per serving: calories 320; fat 20g; protein 30g; carbs 5g; fiber 2g

SEA BASS WITH MEDITERRANEAN SPICE RUB

INGREDIENTS

4 sea bass fillets (about 6 oz each)

2 Tbsp olive oil

1 tsp paprika

1 tsp dried oregano

1/2 tsp ground cumin

1/2 tsp garlic powder

1/4 tsp salt

1/4 tsp black pepper

1 lemon, sliced for garnish

Fresh parsley, chopped (for garnish

DIRECTIONS

- In a small bowl, mix paprika, oregano, cumin, garlic powder, salt, and pepper to create the spice rub.
- Brush each sea bass fillet with olive oil and generously apply the spice rub on both sides.
- Preheat the air fryer to 390°F (200°C).
- Place the sea bass fillets in the air fryer basket in a single layer.
- Cook for 8-10 minutes or until the fish is flaky and cooked through.
- Garnish with lemon slices and sprinkle chopped parsley over the top before serving.

Per serving: calories 210; fat 10g; protein 28g; carbs 1g; fiber 0g

CAJUN SHRIMP

INGREDIENTS

1 lb shrimp, peeled and
deveined

1 Tbsp Cajun seasoning

1 Tbsp olive oil

Lemon wedges for serving

DIRECTIONS

- Toss shrimp with Cajun seasoning and olive oil.
- Cook in the air fryer 400°F (204°C) for 6-8 minutes.
- Serve with lemon wedges.

Per serving: calories 165; fat 6g; protein 24g; carbs 2g; fiber 0g

AIR-FRIED SCALLOPS WITH LEMON BUTTER SAUCE

INGREDIENTS

1 lb sea scallops, side muscle
removed

2 Tbsp olive oil

Salt and pepper, to taste

4 Tbsp butter

1 lemon, juiced

1 clove garlic, minced

1 Tbsp fresh parsley, chopped

DIRECTIONS

- Pat the scallops dry with paper towels. Season with salt and pepper and drizzle with olive oil.
- Preheat the air fryer to 390°F (200°C).
- Arrange scallops in a single layer in the air fryer basket.
- Cook for 3 minutes, flip the scallops, and cook for 3 minutes or until they are opaque and slightly firm to the touch.
- While scallops are cooking, melt butter in a small saucepan over medium heat. Add garlic and sauté until fragrant, about 1 minute. Remove from heat and stir in lemon juice and parsley.
- Serve scallops drizzled with the lemon butter sauce.

Per serving: calories 230; fat 17g; protein 14g; carbs 4g; fiber 0g

SWEET CHILI SHRIMP

INGREDIENTS

1 lb shrimp, peeled and deveined

1/4 cup sweet chili sauce

1 Tbsp soy sauce

1 tsp garlic, minced

Sesame seeds for garnish

DIRECTIONS

- Toss shrimp with sweet chili sauce, soy sauce, and garlic.
- Cook in the air fryer at 400°F (204°C) for 6-8 minutes.
- Garnish with sesame seeds.

Per serving: calories 180; fat 2g; protein 25g; carbs 13g; fiber 0g

SPICED COD WITH CHICKPEAS

INGREDIENTS

4 cod fillets (about 6 oz each)

1 can (15 oz) chickpeas, drained and rinsed

1 tsp paprika

1 tsp cumin

1/2 tsp turmeric

1/2 tsp garlic powder

1/4 tsp cayenne pepper (optional for heat)

2 Tbsp olive oil

Salt and pepper, to taste

1 lemon, sliced

Fresh cilantro, chopped (for garnish

DIRECTIONS

- In a small bowl, mix paprika, cumin, turmeric, garlic powder, cayenne pepper, salt, and pepper.
- Rub the spice mix over the cod fillets evenly.
- Toss chickpeas with half of the olive oil and a pinch of the spice mix.
- Preheat the air fryer to 400°F (204°C).
- Place the spiced cod fillets in the air fryer basket and scatter the spiced chickpeas around them.
- Drizzle the remaining olive oil over the cod and chickpeas.
- Cook for 10-12 minutes until the cod is cooked through and flakes easily with a fork.
- Serve the cod and chickpeas with fresh lemon slices and garnish with chopped cilantro.

Per serving: calories 280; fat 10g; protein 35g; carbs 15g; fiber 4g

MEDITERRANEAN STUFFED MUSSELS

SERVES 4 | PREP 20 MIN | COOK 6-8 MIN

INGREDIENTS

24 large mussels, cleaned and debearded

1/2 cup breadcrumbs

1/4 cup Parmesan cheese, grated

2 cloves garlic, minced

1/4 cup fresh parsley, chopped

1/4 cup fresh basil, chopped

2 Tbsp olive oil

1 lemon, juiced

Salt and pepper, to taste

Lemon wedges, for serving

DIRECTIONS

- Steam mussels in a covered skillet with water until they open. Remove from heat and discard any that do not open. Allow to cool slightly, then remove one shell from each mussel, keeping the mussel attached to the other shell.
- In a bowl, mix breadcrumbs, Parmesan, garlic, parsley, basil, olive oil, lemon juice, salt, and pepper to form the stuffing mixture.
- Preheat the air fryer to 375°F (190°C).
- Spoon the stuffing mixture onto each mussel, pressing gently to adhere.
- Place the stuffed mussels in the air fryer basket in a single layer.
- Cook for 10 minutes or until the topping is golden and crispy.
- Serve immediately with lemon wedges on the side.

CRISPY COD CAKES

SERVES 4 | PREP 10 MIN | COOK 6 MIN

INGREDIENTS

1 lb cod, cooked and flaked

1/2 cup breadcrumbs

1/4 cup mayonnaise

1 egg

2 Tbsp chives, chopped

1 Tbsp Dijon mustard

Salt and pepper to taste

DIRECTIONS

- Mix cod, breadcrumbs, mayonnaise, egg, chives, mustard, salt, and pepper.
- Form into patties.
- Cook in the air fryer at 390°F (200°C) for 6 minutes, flipping halfway through.

Per serving: calories 240; fat 14g; protein 21g; carbs 9g; fiber 1g

LEMON HERB COD

INGREDIENTS

4 cod fillets (6 oz each)

2 Tbsp olive oil

1 Tbsp fresh herbs (parsley, dill, thyme), chopped

1 lemon, juiced and zested

Salt and pepper to taste

DIRECTIONS

- Season cod with salt, pepper, lemon zest, and juice.
- Drizzle with olive oil and sprinkle with herbs.
- Cook in the air fryer at 400°F (204°C) for 10-13 minutes.

Per serving: calories 190; fat 7g; protein 31g; carbs 1g; fiber 0g

TILAPIA WITH CAPER LEMON BUTTER

INGREDIENTS

4 tilapia fillets (6 oz each)

2 Tbsp butter, melted

1 Tbsp capers, drained

1 lemon, juiced

DIRECTIONS

- Season tilapia with salt and pepper.
- Mix butter, capers, and lemon juice.
- Drizzle over tilapia.
- Cook in the air fryer at 400°F (204°C) for 8 minutes.

Per serving: calories 180; fat 9g; protein 23g; carbs 1g; fiber 0g

PESTO SHRIMP WITH ZUCCHINI NOODLES

SERVES 4 | PREP 15 MIN | COOK 6-8 MIN

INGREDIENTS

1 lb large shrimp, peeled and deveined

1/4 cup pesto sauce, homemade or store-bought

4 medium zucchinis, spiralized into noodles

2 tablespoons olive oil

Salt and pepper, to taste

1/4 cup cherry tomatoes, halved (optional)

Grated Parmesan cheese, for garnish

Fresh basil leaves, for garnish

DIRECTIONS

- Marinate the Shrimp:
- In a bowl, toss the shrimp with the pesto sauce. Let marinate for about 10 minutes while you prepare the rest of the ingredients.
- Prepare Zucchini Noodles:
- Heat 1 tablespoon of olive oil in a large skillet over medium heat.
- Add the zucchini noodles and sauté for 2-3 minutes until tender. Season with salt and pepper to taste. Be careful not to overcook to keep them al dente. Remove from heat and set aside.
- Air Fry the Shrimp:
- Preheat the air fryer to 400°F (204°C)
- Place the marinated shrimp in the air fryer basket in a single layer. Cook for 6-8 minutes or until the shrimp are pink and cooked.
- Combine and Serve:
- Toss the cooked shrimp with the zucchini noodles. If using, add the cherry tomatoes.
- Serve the dish garnished with grated Parmesan and fresh basil leaves.

Per serving: calories 240; fat 14g; protein 24g; carbs 6g; fiber 2g

HERB FISH CAKES

INGREDIENTS

1 lb white fish fillets (such as cod, tilapia, or haddock), cooked and flaked

1 cup mashed potatoes

1/4 cup green onions, finely chopped

2 Tbsp fresh parsley, chopped

1 Tbsp fresh dill, chopped

1 Tbsp fresh basil, chopped

1 egg, beaten

1/2 tsp salt

1/4 tsp black pepper

1 cup panko breadcrumbs

Olive oil spray

DIRECTIONS

- In a large bowl, mix the flaked fish, mashed potatoes, green onions, parsley, dill, basil, egg, salt, and pepper until well combined.
- Shape the mixture into 8 patties.
- Place the panko breadcrumbs in a shallow dish and coat each patty evenly.
- Preheat the air fryer to 400°F (204°C). Spray the air fryer basket with olive oil spray.
- Place the fish cakes in the basket, ensuring they do not touch. Spray the tops with olive oil.
- Cook for 5 minutes; flip the fish cakes, spray the other side with olive oil, and cook for another 5 minutes or until golden brown and crispy.
- Serve the fish cakes with a side of tartar sauce or a squeeze of fresh lemon.

Per serving: calories 230; fat 4g; protein 23g; carbs 24g; fiber 1g

TILAPIA WITH OLIVE TAPENADE

SERVES 4 | PREP 5 MIN | COOK 8 MIN

INGREDIENTS

4 tilapia fillets (6 oz each)

1/4 cup olive tapenade

1 Tbsp olive oil

1/2 lemon, sliced

Salt and pepper to taste

DIRECTIONS

- Season tilapia with salt and pepper.
- Spread tapenade over each fillet.
- Top with lemon slices.
- Drizzle with olive oil.
- Cook in the air fryer at 400°F (204°C) for 8 minutes.

Per serving: calories 200; fat 10g; protein 26g; carbs 2g; fiber 1g

HALIBUT WITH GARLIC LEMON AIOLI

SERVES 4 | PREP 10 MIN | COOK 8-10 MIN

INGREDIENTS

4 halibut fillets (6 oz each)

2 Tbsp olive oil

1 Tbsp garlic, minced

2 Tbsp mayonnaise

1 lemon, juiced and zested

Salt and pepper to taste

DIRECTIONS

- Mix mayonnaise, lemon juice, zest, and garlic to make aioli.
- Brush halibut with olive oil and season with salt and pepper.
- Cook in the air fryer at 390°F (200°C) for 8-10 minutes.
- Serve with garlic lemon aioli.

Per serving: calories 230; fat 12g; protein 28g; carbs 2g; fiber 0g

CHICKEN & TURKEY

Tips from the Author

"Marinate your poultry to infuse it with flavor before air frying. The high heat of the air fryer locks in moisture, ensuring your chicken and turkey remain juicy and tender. Experiment with different marinades and enjoy the delicious results."

MEDITERRANEAN HERB CHICKEN

SERVES 4 | PREP 15 MIN | COOK 20 MIN

INGREDIENTS

4 boneless, skinless chicken breasts

2 tablespoons olive oil

1 lemon, zested and juiced

3 cloves garlic, minced

1 tablespoon fresh rosemary, chopped

1 tablespoon fresh thyme, chopped

1 tablespoon fresh oregano, chopped

Salt and pepper, to taste

Fresh parsley, chopped (for garnish)

DIRECTIONS

- Mix olive oil and lemon with all spices, salt, and pepper in a bowl to create a marinade.
- Coat the chicken thoroughly and refrigerate for 30 minutes to 2 hours.
- Preheat the air fryer to 375°F (190°C). Place marinated chicken in a single layer in the air fryer basket.
- Cook the chicken for 20 minutes, flipping halfway through, until it reaches an internal temperature of 165°F (74°C) and is golden.
- Garnish with fresh parsley before serving, accompanied by roasted vegetables or a fresh salad.

Per serving: calories 220; fat 8g; protein 34g; carbs 3g; fiber 1g

GREEK TURKEY MEATBALLS

SERVES 4 | PREP 15 MIN | COOK 15 MIN

INGREDIENTS

1 lb ground turkey

1/2 cup feta cheese, crumbled

1/4 cup Kalamata olives, finely chopped

1 egg, beaten

1/4 cup breadcrumbs

2 cloves garlic, minced

2 tablespoons fresh parsley, chopped

1 tablespoon fresh oregano, chopped

1 teaspoon onion powder

Salt and pepper, to taste

Olive oil spray

Tzatziki sauce for serving

DIRECTIONS

- In a large bowl, combine ground turkey, feta cheese, Kalamata olives, egg, breadcrumbs, garlic, parsley, oregano, onion powder, salt, and pepper. Mix until well combined.
- Shape the mixture into small, round meatballs about 1 inch in diameter.
- Preheat the air fryer to 375°F (190°C). Lightly spray the air fryer basket with olive oil.
- Place the meatballs in the air fryer basket, ensuring they do not touch to allow for even cooking.
- Air fry for 15 minutes, turning halfway through or until the meatballs are golden and cooked.
- Serve the meatballs with tzatziki sauce on the side.

Per serving: calories 290; fat 15g; protein 28g; carbs 8g; fiber 1g

SHAWARMA-STYLE CHICKEN

INGREDIENTS

1 lb chicken breasts, thinly sliced

2 tbsp olive oil

Juice of 1 lemon

1 tbsp shawarma spice blend (combine ground cumin, coriander, paprika, turmeric, garlic powder, salt, pepper, and a pinch of cayenne)

4 cloves garlic, minced

Salt and pepper, to taste

Garlic sauce, for serving

DIRECTIONS

- In a bowl, mix olive oil, lemon juice, shawarma spices, garlic, salt, and pepper. Add the chicken slices and coat well with the marinade. Refrigerate for at least 1 hour or overnight for best results.
- Preheat the air fryer to 360°F (182°C).
- Place the marinated chicken slices in the air fryer basket. Cook for 12-15 minutes, flipping halfway through, until the chicken is cooked through and slightly crispy.
- Serve the chicken with garlic sauce on the side.

Per serving: calories 275; fat 11g; protein 34g; carbs 4g; fiber 1g

TURKISH CHICKEN KEBABS

SERVES 4 | PREP 15 MIN | COOK 15 MIN

INGREDIENTS

1 lb chicken breast, cut into chunks

1/2 cup plain yogurt

2 tablespoons olive oil

1 tablespoon paprika

3 cloves garlic, minced

1 teaspoon ground cumin

1/2 teaspoon salt

1/4 teaspoon black pepper

Fresh cilantro or parsley, chopped (for garnish)

Lemon wedges for serving

DIRECTIONS

- Combine yogurt, olive oil, paprika, garlic, cumin, salt, and pepper in a bowl to make a marinade.
- Add chicken chunks to the bowl and toss to coat with the marinade. Cover and refrigerate for at least 1 hour or overnight.
- Thread the chicken onto skewers and air fry at 360°F (182°C) for 12-15 minutes, turning halfway through.
- Garnish with cilantro or parsley and serve with lemon wedges.
- Enjoy your tasty chicken skewers!

Per serving: calories 225; fat 10g; protein 30g; carbs 3g; fiber 1g

CHICKEN PARMESAN

INGREDIENTS

4 boneless, skinless chicken breasts

1/2 cup all-purpose flour

2 large eggs, beaten

1 cup breadcrumbs

1/2 cup grated Parmesan cheese

1 teaspoon garlic powder

1 teaspoon Italian seasoning

Salt and pepper, to taste

1 cup marinara sauce

1 cup shredded mozzarella cheese

Olive oil spray

Fresh basil for garnish

DIRECTIONS

- Mix breadcrumbs, Parmesan cheese, garlic powder, Italian seasoning, salt, and pepper in a bowl.
- Coat chicken in flour, eggs, and the breadcrumb mixture.
- Spray the air fryer basket with olive oil, add chicken, and spray the tops with oil.
- Air fry at 375°F (190°C) for 10 minutes, then flip and cook for another 5.
- Top with marinara sauce and mozzarella cheese, and cook for 5 more minutes until cheese is melted.
- Garnish with fresh basil and serve. Enjoy!

Per serving: calories 450; fat 18g; protein 40g; carbs 30g; fiber 2g

LEMON GARLIC TURKEY BREASTS

SERVES 4 | PREP 15 MIN | COOK 20 MIN

INGREDIENTS

4 turkey breast cutlets (about 1 lb)

1/4 cup olive oil

Juice of 2 lemons

4 cloves garlic, minced

1 tablespoon fresh rosemary, chopped

1 tablespoon fresh thyme, chopped

Salt and pepper, to taste

Lemon slices and fresh herbs for garnish

DIRECTIONS

- In a bowl, whisk together olive oil, lemon juice, minced garlic, rosemary, thyme, salt, and pepper to make the marinade.

- Place turkey cutlets in a resealable plastic bag or shallow dish and pour the marinade over them. Ensure all pieces are evenly coated. Refrigerate and let marinate for at least 30 minutes, preferably a few hours.

- Preheat the air fryer to 360°F (182°C).

- Remove turkey from marinade and place in the air fryer basket. Do not overcrowd. Cook in batches if necessary.

- Air fry for 10 minutes, then flip the cutlets and continue cooking for another 10 minutes, or until the turkey is cooked through and reaches an internal temperature of 165°F (74°C).

- Garnish with lemon slices and additional fresh herbs before serving.

Per serving: calories 215; fat 9g; protein 29g; carbs 2g; fiber 0g

CHICKEN AND ARTICHOKE HEARTS

INGREDIENTS

8 chicken thighs, boneless and skinless

1 can (14 oz) artichoke hearts, drained and halved

1/4 cup capers, drained

1 lemon, sliced

2 tablespoons olive oil

2 cloves garlic, minced

1 teaspoon dried oregano

Salt and pepper, to taste

Fresh parsley, chopped (for garnish)

DIRECTIONS

- In a large bowl, combine olive oil, garlic, oregano, salt, and pepper. Add chicken thighs and toss to coat evenly.
- Preheat the air fryer to 380°F (193°C).
- Arrange the seasoned chicken thighs in the air fryer basket. Scatter artichoke hearts, capers, and lemon slices around the chicken.
- Air fry for 20 minutes, or until the chicken is golden brown and reaches an internal temperature of 165°F (74°C), turning halfway through cooking.
- Garnish with fresh parsley before serving.

Per serving: calories 320; fat 22g; protein 26g; carbs 4g; fiber 2g

SPICED TURKEY PATTIES

INGREDIENTS

- 1 lb ground turkey
- 2 teaspoons ground cumin
- 2 teaspoons ground coriander
- 1/4 cup fresh parsley, finely chopped
- 1/4 cup fresh cilantro, finely chopped
- 1 small onion, finely chopped
- 2 cloves garlic, minced
- Salt and pepper, to taste
- Olive oil spray

DIRECTIONS

- In a bowl, combine ground turkey, cumin, coriander, parsley, cilantro, onion, garlic, salt, and pepper. Mix well until all ingredients are evenly distributed.
- Form the mixture into 4-6 patties, depending on your preferred size.
- Preheat the air fryer to 360°F (182°C).
- Lightly spray the air fryer basket with olive oil. Place the patties in the basket, ensuring they don't touch each other.
- Air fry for 15 minutes, flipping halfway through or until the patties are fully cooked and have reached an internal temperature of 165°F (74°C).
- Serve the patties warm, with your choice of side dishes, or in a burger bun with toppings.

Per serving: calories 180; fat 10g; protein 20g; carbs 3g; fiber 1g

CHICKEN SOUVLAKI

INGREDIENTS

1 lb chicken breast, cut into 1-inch cubes

1/4 cup olive oil

Juice of 1 lemon

3 cloves garlic, minced

2 teaspoons dried oregano

1 bell pepper, cut into 1-inch pieces

1 large onion, cut into wedges

Salt and pepper, to taste

Fresh parsley or oregano for garnish

DIRECTIONS

- In a large bowl, whisk together olive oil, lemon juice, garlic, oregano, salt, and pepper to make the marinade.
- Add the chicken cubes to the marinade, mixing well to ensure each piece is coated. Cover and refrigerate for at least 1 hour, preferably longer, to enhance the flavors.
- Preheat the air fryer to 400°F (200°C).
- Thread the marinated chicken, bell pepper, and onion alternately onto skewers.
- Place the skewers in the air fryer basket and cook for about 15 minutes, turning halfway through or until the chicken is fully cooked and the vegetables are tender.
- Garnish with fresh parsley or oregano before serving.

Per serving: calories 250; fat 14g; protein 27g; carbs 6g; fiber 2g

PAPRIKA AND LIME CHICKEN DRUMSTICKS

INGREDIENTS

8 chicken drumsticks

2 tablespoons olive oil

2 teaspoons smoked paprika

Zest of 2 limes

Juice of 1 lime

2 cloves garlic, minced

1 teaspoon salt

1/2 teaspoon black pepper

Fresh cilantro, chopped (for garnish)

Lime wedges for serving

DIRECTIONS

- Combine olive oil, smoked paprika, lime zest, lime juice, minced garlic, salt, and pepper to create the marinade.
- Add the chicken drumsticks and toss to coat evenly. Cover and refrigerate for at least 30 mins or overnight.
- Preheat the air fryer to 400°F (200°C).
- Place the marinated drumsticks in the air fryer basket.
- Air fry for 20 minutes, turning halfway through, until the chicken is crispy on the outside and cooked through.
- Garnish with cilantro and serve with lime wedges.

Per serving: calories 310; fat 18g; protein 34g; carbs 2g; fiber 1g

ZA'ATAR CHICKEN THIGHS

SERVES 4 | PREP 10 MIN | COOK 20 MIN

INGREDIENTS

8 chicken thighs, bone-in and skin-on

3 tablespoons za'atar seasoning

2 tablespoons olive oil

Salt and pepper, to taste

Lemon wedges for serving

DIRECTIONS

- In a small bowl, mix za'atar seasoning, olive oil, salt, and pepper to create a paste.
- Rub the za'atar paste evenly over the chicken thighs.
- Preheat the air fryer to 380°F (193°C).
- Place the chicken thighs in the air fryer basket, skin side down. Do not overcrowd the basket; cook in batches if necessary.
- Air fry for 10 minutes, then flip the thighs so the skin side is up, and continue cooking for another 10 minutes or until the chicken is golden brown and crispy.
- Serve the chicken thighs hot, garnished with lemon wedges.

Per serving: calories 310; fat 22g; protein 24g; carbs 1g; fiber 0g

MOROCCAN CHICKEN WINGS

SERVES 4 | PREP 10 MIN | COOK 20 MIN

INGREDIENTS

2 lbs chicken wings, tips removed, and wings split at the joint

2 tablespoons olive oil

1 tablespoon ground cumin

1 tablespoon smoked paprika

1 teaspoon ground coriander

1 teaspoon ground cinnamon

1/2 teaspoon ground ginger

1/2 teaspoon cayenne pepper (adjust based on heat preference)

Salt and pepper, to taste

DIRECTIONS

- Mix olive oil, cumin, smoked paprika, coriander, cinnamon, ginger, cayenne pepper, salt, and pepper in a large bowl.
- Add the chicken wings and toss to coat. Marinate for 30 mins in the fridge (or overnight for more flavor)
- Preheat the air fryer to 400°F (200°C). Arrange the wings in a single layer and cook for 20 mins, turning halfway.
- Garnish with cilantro and serve with lemon wedges.

Per serving: calories 290; fat 20g; protein 24g; carbs 2g; fiber 1g

TURKEY AND SPINACH PINWHEELS

SERVES 4 | PREP 15 MIN | COOK 10 MIN

INGREDIENTS

4 large turkey breast slices, thinly sliced

1 cup fresh spinach, finely chopped

1/2 cup cream cheese, softened

1/4 cup grated Parmesan cheese

1 garlic clove, minced

Salt and pepper, to taste

Olive oil spray

DIRECTIONS

- Lay out the turkey breast slices on a flat surface. Pound slices if too thick.
- Mix spinach, cream cheese, Parmesan cheese, and garlic. Season with salt and pepper.
- Spread the spinach and cheese mixture evenly over each turkey slice.
- Roll up tightly and secure with toothpicks.
- Air fry for 10 mins at 375°F (190°C) or until the turkey is cooked and the outside is slightly crispy.
- Remove from the air fryer, slice into pinwheels, and serve.

Per serving: calories 200; fat 10g; protein 25g; carbs 3g; fiber 1g

MEDITERRANEAN STUFFED CHICKEN

SERVES 4 | PREP 20 MIN | COOK 25 MIN

INGREDIENTS

4 chicken breasts, boneless and skinless

1 cup fresh spinach, chopped

1/2 cup sun-dried tomatoes, chopped

1/2 cup feta cheese, crumbled

2 cloves garlic, minced

Salt and pepper, to taste

2 tablespoons olive oil

Fresh basil for garnish

DIRECTIONS

- Preheat the air fryer to 375°F (190°C).
- Cut a side of each chicken breast to create a pocket.
- Mix spinach, sun-dried tomatoes, feta, garlic, salt, and pepper in a bowl.
- Stuff the mixture into each chicken breast.
- Brush the chicken with olive oil and season with salt and pepper.
- Place chicken in the air fryer basket, ensuring they do not touch.
- Air fry for 22-25 minutes until cooked through.
- Garnish with basil and serve.

Per serving: calories 300; fat 15g; protein 35g; carbs 8g; fiber 2g

CRISPY DIJON CHICKEN

SERVES 4 | PREP 10 MIN | COOK 20 MIN

INGREDIENTS

- 8 chicken drumsticks
- 1/2 cup Dijon mustard
- 1 cup breadcrumbs
- Salt and pepper, to taste
- Olive oil spray

DIRECTIONS

- Preheat the air fryer to 375°F (190°C).
- Coat each drumstick with Dijon mustard.
- Season the breadcrumbs with salt and pepper, then roll the mustard-coated drumsticks in the breadcrumbs until fully covered.
- Spray the air fryer basket with olive oil. Place the drumsticks in the basket, making sure they are not touching.
- Air fry for 20 minutes, turning halfway through, until the chicken is crispy and cooked through.
- Serve hot.

Per serving: calories 310; fat 15g; protein 27g; carbs 15g; fiber 1g

TURKEY AND VEGETABLE SKEWERS

SERVES 4 | PREP 15 MIN | COOK 15 MIN

INGREDIENTS

1 lb turkey breast, cut into cubes

1 red bell pepper, cut into 1-inch pieces

1 zucchini, cut into 1-inch slices

1 yellow squash, cut into 1-inch slices

1 onion, cut into wedges

1/4 cup olive oil

2 cloves garlic, minced

1 lemon, juiced

1 tablespoon dried oregano

Salt and pepper, to taste

Fresh parsley for garnish

DIRECTIONS

- Mix olive oil, garlic, lemon juice, oregano, salt, and pepper in a large bowl.
- Add the turkey cubes and vegetables to coat with the marinade. Let marinate for 30 mins in the fridge.
- Preheat the air fryer to 400°F (200°C).
- Thread the turkey and vegetables onto skewers.
- Place the skewers in the air fryer basket.
- Air fry for 15 minutes, turning halfway through.
- Garnish with fresh parsley before serving.

Per serving: calories 275; fat 14g; protein 28g; carbs 8g; fiber 2g

CHICKEN AND OLIVE TAGINE

INGREDIENTS

4 chicken thighs, bone-in and skin-on

1 cup green olives, pitted

1 preserved lemon, thinly sliced

1 onion, sliced

2 cloves garlic, minced

1 teaspoon ground cumin

1 teaspoon ground coriander

1/2 teaspoon ground ginger

1/2 teaspoon paprika

1/4 teaspoon saffron threads (optional)

2 tablespoons olive oil

Salt and pepper, to taste

Fresh cilantro, chopped for garnish

DIRECTIONS

- In a large bowl, combine olive oil, cumin, coriander, ginger, paprika, saffron, salt, and pepper. Add chicken thighs and toss to coat evenly.

- Place the seasoned chicken in the air fryer basket. Add sliced onions, garlic, preserved lemons, and olives around the chicken.

- Pour chicken broth over the ingredients in the basket.

- Cook in the air fryer at 360°F (182°C) for 25 minutes, or until the chicken is fully cooked and the onions are tender.

- Garnish with chopped cilantro before serving.

Per serving: calories 400; fat 28g; protein 30g; carbs 8g; fiber 2g

GARLIC AND HERB TURKEY TENDERLOIN

SERVES 4 | PREP 10 MIN | COOK 20 MIN

INGREDIENTS

1 turkey tenderloin (about 1 lb)

3 cloves garlic, minced

1/4 cup fresh parsley, finely chopped

1 tablespoon fresh rosemary, chopped

1 tablespoon fresh thyme, chopped

2 tablespoons olive oil

Salt and pepper, to taste

Lemon wedges for serving

DIRECTIONS

- Mix olive oil, minced garlic, parsley, rosemary, thyme, salt, and pepper to create the marinade.
- Place the turkey tenderloin in a resealable plastic bag or shallow dish and pour the marinade over it. Ensure the tenderloin is well-coated. Seal the bag or cover the dish and marinate for at least 30 mins.
- Preheat the air fryer to 360°F (182°C).
- Remove the turkey tenderloin from the marinade and place it in the air fryer basket.
- Air fry for 20 mins, turning halfway, cook until the turkey is cooked through and reaches an internal temperature of 165°F (74°C).
- Let the turkey rest for a few minutes before slicing.
- Serve with lemon wedges.

Per serving: calories 180; fat 8g; protein 26g; carbs 1g; fiber 0g

CHICKEN CAPRESE

INGREDIENTS

4 boneless, skinless chicken breasts

4 slices fresh mozzarella cheese

2 tomatoes, sliced

Fresh basil leaves

2 tablespoons olive oil

Salt and pepper, to taste

Balsamic glaze (optional for drizzling)

DIRECTIONS

- Preheat the air fryer to 360°F (182°C).
- Brush chicken breasts with olive oil and season with salt and pepper.
- Place chicken in the air fryer basket and cook for 10 minutes.
- Remove the basket and top each chicken breast with tomato slices, a slice of mozzarella, and a few basil leaves.
- Return to the air fryer and cook for another 5 minutes and the cheese is bubbly and slightly golden.
- Serve hot, drizzled with balsamic glaze if desired.

Per serving: calories 300; fat 16g; protein 35g; carbs 4g; fiber 1g

GREEK CHICKEN PITAS

INGREDIENTS

4 boneless, skinless chicken breasts

2 tablespoons olive oil

1 tablespoon Greek seasoning

4 pita breads

1 cup Greek salad (combination of chopped cucumbers, tomatoes, red onions, and Kalamata olives)

1/2 cup tzatziki sauce

Salt and pepper, to taste

Fresh lemon juice (optional)

DIRECTIONS

- Combine olive oil, Greek seasoning, salt, and pepper in a bowl. Add chicken breasts and toss to coat evenly. Let marinate for at least 15 mins.
- Preheat the air fryer to 360°F (182°C). Place marinated chicken in air fryer and cook for 18-20 minutes, flipping halfway.
- Once cooked, let the chicken rest for a few minutes before slicing it into strips.
- Warm the pita breads in the air fryer for 1-2 mins.
- Assemble the pitas by adding a layer of Greek salad, chicken strips, and a dollop of tzatziki to each pita. Drizzle with fresh lemon juice.
- Fold the pitas and serve immediately.

Per serving: calories 450; fat 18g; protein 30g; carbs 40g; fiber 5g

BEEF, LAMB & PORK

Tips from the Author

"Use your air fryer to achieve a perfect sear on beef, lamb, and pork. Start with a high temperature to create a delicious crust, then lower it to cook through. Don't forget to let the meat rest after cooking for maximum juiciness."

BEEF KOFTA KEBABS

SERVES 4 | PREP 20 MIN | COOK 15 MIN

INGREDIENTS

1 lb ground beef

1 onion, finely grated

3 cloves garlic, minced

2 Tbsp fresh parsley, chopped

1 Tbsp ground cumin

1 tsp ground coriander

1/2 tsp ground cinnamon

1/2 tsp cayenne pepper

Salt and pepper, to taste

Olive oil spray

DIRECTIONS

- Combine ground beef, onion, garlic, parsley, cumin, coriander, cinnamon, cayenne, salt, and pepper in a large bowl and mix well.
- Shape the mixture into elongated kebabs around skewers.
- Preheat the air fryer to 360°F (182°C).
- Spray the air fryer basket with olive oil. Place kebabs in the basket.
- Air fry for 15 minutes, turning halfway through, until fully cooked.

Per serving: calories 320; fat 20g; protein 27g; carbs 5g; fiber 1g

MEDITERRANEAN BEEF PATTIES

SERVES 4 | PREP 15 MIN | COOK 15 MIN

INGREDIENTS

1 lb ground beef

1/4 cup sun-dried tomatoes, chopped

1/4 cup Kalamata olives, chopped

2 Tbsp fresh herbs (such as parsley and oregano), chopped

1/2 cup feta cheese, crumbled

1 garlic clove, minced

Salt and pepper, to taste

Olive oil spray

Tzatziki sauce for serving

DIRECTIONS

- In a large bowl, mix ground beef, sun-dried tomatoes, olives, herbs, feta cheese, and garlic. Season with salt and pepper.
- Form the mixture into patties.
- Preheat the air fryer to 375°F (190°C). Lightly spray the air fryer basket with olive oil. Place the patties in the basket.
- Cook for 15 minutes, flipping halfway through, until the patties are browned and cooked.
- Serve the patties with tzatziki sauce.

Per serving: calories 290; fat 20g; protein 22g; carbs 5g; fiber 1g

STUFFED BELL PEPPERS

SERVES 4 | PREP 20 MIN | COOK 30 MIN

INGREDIENTS

4 large bell peppers, tops cut off and seeds removed
1 lb ground beef
1 cup cooked rice
1 can (14.5 oz) diced tomatoes, drained
1 onion, chopped
2 cloves garlic, minced
1 cup shredded cheddar cheese
1 tsp salt
1/2 tsp black pepper
Olive oil spray

DIRECTIONS

- Preheat the air fryer to 350°F (177°C).
- In a skillet over medium heat, cook ground beef with onion and garlic, then add cooked rice, diced tomatoes, salt, and pepper.
- Spoon the mixture into bell peppers and place them in the air fryer basket.
- Cook for 15 minutes, then add shredded cheese.
- Cook for another 15 minutes until peppers are tender and cheese is melted

Per serving: calories 450; fat 22g; protein 26g; carbs 34g; fiber 4g

MEDITERRANEAN BEEF STEAK

SERVES 4 | PREP 10 MIN | COOK 10 MIN

INGREDIENTS

4 beef steaks (such as sirloin or ribeye), about 6 ounces each
2 Tbsp olive oil
2 cloves garlic, minced
1 tsp dried oregano
1 tsp dried thyme
1 tsp dried rosemary
Juice of 1 lemon
Salt and pepper, to taste
Fresh parsley, chopped (for garnish)

DIRECTIONS

- In a small bowl, mix olive oil, garlic, oregano, thyme, rosemary, lemon juice, salt, and pepper. Rub this marinade over the steaks and let them sit for at least 30 mins or overnight.
- Preheat the air fryer to 400°F (200°C).
- Air fryer steaks for about 10 mins for medium-rare, or adjust the time to your preferred doneness, turning halfway through the cooking time.
- Rest the steaks for a few minutes after cooking, then garnish with fresh parsley before serving.

Per serving: calories 350; fat 20g; protein 34g; carbs 1g; fiber 0g

BEEF AND FETA STUFFED ZUCCHINI

SERVES 4 | PREP 15 MIN | COOK 20 MIN

INGREDIENTS

4 medium zucchinis, halved lengthwise and scooped out to create boats

1 lb ground beef

1/2 cup feta cheese, crumbled

1 small onion, finely chopped

2 cloves garlic, minced

1 teaspoon dried oregano

1/2 teaspoon dried basil

Salt and pepper, to taste

Olive oil spray

Fresh parsley

DIRECTIONS

- In a skillet over medium heat, cook the ground beef with onion and garlic until the beef is thoroughly browned. Drain excess grease.
- Stir in oregano, basil, salt, and pepper. Remove from heat and mix in the crumbled feta cheese.
- Spoon the mixture into the scooped-out zucchini boats.
- Air fry for about 15-20 minutes at 375°F (190°C) until the zucchini is tender.
- Garnish with fresh parsley before serving.

Per serving: calories 350; fat 22g; protein 28g; carbs 8g; fiber 2g

SHAWARMA-STYLE BEEF

SERVES 4 | PREP 15 MIN + Marinating | COOK 20 MIN

INGREDIENTS

1 lb beef sirloin, thinly sliced

2 Tbsp olive oil

Juice of 1 lemon

3 cloves garlic, minced

1 Tbsp ground cumin

1 Tbsp smoked paprika

1 tsp turmeric

1/2 tsp ground cinnamon

1/2 tsp ground cloves

1/2 tsp ground coriander

Salt and pepper

Fresh parsley

DIRECTIONS

- In a bowl, mix olive oil, lemon juice, garlic, cumin, paprika, turmeric, cinnamon, cloves, coriander, salt, and pepper to create the marinade.
- Add the thinly sliced beef to the marinade and let marinate for at least 2 hours in the fridge.
- Air fryer for 15-20 mins at 400°F (200°C) until the beef is fully cooked.
- Garnish with fresh parsley and serve.
- Enjoy with fresh pita, vegetables, or a creamy sauce for a complete meal.

Per serving: calories 300; fat 15g; protein 25g; carbs 5g; fiber 1g

SMOKY ESPRESSO STEAK

INGREDIENTS

4 beef steaks (such as sirloin), about 1 inch thick

2 Tbsp finely ground espresso

1 Tbsp smoked paprika

1 Tbsp brown sugar

1 tsp garlic powder

1 tsp onion powder

1/2 tsp cayenne pepper

Salt and black pepper, to taste

Olive oil

DIRECTIONS

- Mix espresso, smoked paprika, brown sugar, garlic powder, onion powder, cayenne, salt, and pepper to make the rub.
- Brush steaks with oil and apply rub. Marinate for 30 minutes.
- Preheat air fryer to 400°F (200°C).
- Air fry steaks for 10 minutes, flipping once.
- Rest steaks briefly before serving.

Per serving: calories 400; fat 25g; protein 38g; carbs 2g; fiber 0.5g

BEEF SOUVLAKI

INGREDIENTS

1 lb beef sirloin, cut into 1-inch cubes

2 Tbsp olive oil

Juice of 1 lemon

3 cloves garlic, minced

2 tsp dried oregano

Salt and pepper, to taste

1 bell pepper, cut into 1-inch pieces (optional)

1 onion, cut into 1-inch pieces (optional)

Fresh parsley or oregano for garnish

DIRECTIONS

- Combine olive oil, lemon juice, garlic, oregano, salt, and pepper to create a marinade.
- Add beef cubes to the marinade and mix well. Refrigerate for at least 2 hours or overnight.
- Preheat the air fryer to 400°F (200°C).
- Thread marinated beef, bell peppers, and onions onto skewers.
- Place skewers in the air fryer and cook for 10 minutes, turning halfway through, until beef is cooked.
- Garnish with fresh herbs and serve.

Per serving: calories 310; fat 18g; protein 26g; carbs 5g; fiber 1g

MEDITERRANEAN BEEF TACOS

INGREDIENTS

1 lb ground beef

1 tsp smoked paprika, cumin

1/2 tsp coriander

1/4 tsp chili powder

Salt and pepper

8 small corn tortillas

1/2 cup tzatziki sauce

1/2 cup feta cheese, crumbled

1 cup cherry tomatoes, halved

1/2 cup cucumber, diced

1/4 cup red onion, thinly sliced

1/4 cup fresh mint, chopped

1/4 cup fresh parsley, chopped

2 Tbsp olive oil

DIRECTIONS

- In a skillet, cook ground beef, paprika, cumin, coriander, chili powder, salt, and pepper.
- Warm tortillas in the air fryer at 300°F (150°C) for about 1-2 minutes or until heated through.
- Assemble tacos by placing a spoonful of cooked beef on each tortilla. Top with tzatziki sauce, feta cheese, tomatoes, cucumber, red onion, mint, and parsley.

Per serving: calories 450; fat 25g; protein 25g; carbs 35g; fiber 5g

BEEF AND OLIVE EMPANADAS

INGREDIENTS

1 lb ground beef
1/2 cup green olives, pitted and chopped
1 onion, finely chopped
2 cloves garlic, minced
1 tsp smoked paprika
1/2 tsp cumin
Salt and pepper, to taste
1 package of ready-made empanada dough (or homemade dough for empanadas)
1 egg, beaten (for egg wash)

DIRECTIONS

- Sauté onion and garlic in olive oil until soft. Add beef, paprika, cumin, salt, and pepper; cook until browned. Stir in olives.
- Roll out dough, cut into rounds, and fill with the beef mixture. Fold and seal edges with a fork.
- Brush with egg wash and air fry at 350°F (177°C) for 20 minutes until golden.
- Serve warm.

Per serving: calories 450; fat 25g; protein 25g; carbs 35g; fiber 2g

GREEK LAMB MEATBALLS

SERVES 4 | PREP 15 MIN | COOK 20 MIN

INGREDIENTS

- 1 lb ground lamb
- 1/4 cup breadcrumbs
- 1 egg
- 1/4 cup feta cheese, crumbled
- 2 cloves garlic, minced
- 1 small onion, finely chopped
- 2 Tbsp fresh mint, chopped
- 2 Tbsp fresh parsley, chopped
- 1 tsp dried oregano
- 1/2 tsp cumin
- Salt and pepper, to taste
- Olive oil spray

DIRECTIONS

- Mix all ingredients in a bowl.
- Form into 1-inch balls.
- Preheat the air fryer to 375°F (190°C) and lightly spray the basket with olive oil.
- Cook meatballs for 20 minutes, turning halfway.
- Serve warm with tzatziki sauce or a Greek salad

Per serving: calories 330; fat 22g; protein 26g; carbs 8g; fiber 1g

LAMB CHOPS WITH ROSEMARY

SERVES 4 | PREP 15 MIN + Marinating | COOK 12 MIN

INGREDIENTS

- 8 lamb chops
- 2 Tbsp olive oil
- 4 cloves garlic, minced
- 2 Tbsp fresh rosemary, chopped
- Juice of 1 lemon
- Salt and pepper, to taste

DIRECTIONS

- Mix olive oil, garlic, rosemary, lemon juice, salt, and pepper in a bowl.
- Marinate lamb chops in the mixture for at least 2 hours in the fridge.
- Preheat the air fryer to 400°F (200°C) and lightly spray the basket with olive oil.
- Cook lamb chops for 12 minutes, turning halfway.
- Serve warm with a side of grilled vegetables or a fresh Greek salad.

Per serving: calories 310; fat 20g; protein 30g; carbs 2g; fiber 0g

AIR-FRIED LAMB GYROS

SERVES 4 | PREP 15 MIN + Marinating | COOK 10 MIN

INGREDIENTS

1 lb 1 Tbsp dried oregano

2 tsp garlic powder

1 tsp ground cumin

Salt and pepper, to taste

4 pita breads

1 cup Greek yogurt

1 cucumber, diced

1 small red onion, thinly sliced

1 tomato, thinly sliced

Fresh parsley, chopped (for garnish)

lamb, thinly sliced

2 Tbsp olive oil

DIRECTIONS

- Mix olive oil, oregano, garlic powder, cumin, salt, and pepper in a bowl. Marinate lamb in the mixture for at least 1 hour in the fridge.
- Preheat the air fryer to 400°F (200°C) and lightly spray the basket with olive oil.
- Cook lamb slices for 10 minutes, turning halfway.
- Warm pita breads in the air fryer for 1-2 minutes.
- Assemble gyros: Spread Greek yogurt on pitas and add cooked lamb, cucumber, onion, and tomato.
- Serve warm with fresh parsley.

Per serving: calories 460; fat 22g; protein 28g; carbs 35g; fiber 4g

LAMB AND PINE NUT MINI PIES

SERVES 4 | PREP 25 MIN | COOK 15 MIN

INGREDIENTS

1 lb minced lamb

1/2 cup pine nuts, toasted

1 onion, finely chopped

2 cloves garlic, minced

2 tsp ground cumin

1 tsp paprika

1/2 tsp ground cinnamon

Salt and pepper, to taste

1 package of pre-made pie dough or puff pastry

1 egg, beaten (for egg wash)

Olive oil

DIRECTIONS

- Sauté onion and garlic in olive oil until soft. Add lamb and spices; cook until browned. Mix in pine nuts and cool.
- Cut dough into rounds, fill with lamb mixture, and fold and seal edges.
- Brush pies with egg wash.
- Air fry at 375°F (190°C) for 15 minutes until golden.
- Serve warm.

Per serving: calories 580; fat 38g; protein 28g; carbs 35g; fiber 3g

LAMB STUFFED EGGPLANT

INGREDIENTS

2 large eggplants, halved lengthwise
1 lb ground lamb
1 onion, finely chopped
2 cloves garlic, minced
1 tsp ground cumin
1 tsp smoked paprika
1/2 tsp cinnamon
Salt and pepper, to taste
1 cup diced tomatoes (canned or fresh)
1/2 cup shredded mozzarella cheese
Olive oil
Fresh parsley, chopped (for garnish

DIRECTIONS

- Scoop out the centers of the eggplant halves to create a shell.
- Brush with oil, salt, and pepper.
- Brown lamb with onions, garlic, spices, and tomatoes.
- Stuff eggplants with lamb mixture and top with cheese.
- Air fry at 375°F (190°C) for 20-25 minutes.
- Garnish with parsley and serve warm.

Per serving: calories 410; fat 28g; protein 25g; carbs 20g; fiber 8g

LAMB FAJITAS

INGREDIENTS

1 lb lamb, thinly sliced

2 bell peppers (any color), sliced

1 large onion, sliced

2 Tbsp olive oil

Juice of 1 lime

2 tsp chili powder

1 tsp ground cumin

1 tsp smoked paprika

1/2 tsp garlic powder

Salt and pepper, to taste

Tortillas, for serving

DIRECTIONS

- Mix olive oil, lime juice, chili powder, cumin, paprika, garlic powder, salt, and pepper in a bowl. Marinate the lamb slices in this mixture for at least 1 hour.

- Preheat the air fryer to 400°F (200°C).

- Add marinated lamb, peppers, and onions to the air fryer basket.

- Cook for 10 minutes, shaking or stirring halfway through.

- Serve hot on tortillas with your choice of toppings, such as sour cream, salsa, or guacamole.

Per serving: calories 310; fat 18g; protein 25g; carbs 10g; fiber 2g

SPICED LAMB RIBS

INGREDIENTS

2 lbs lamb ribs

2 Tbsp olive oil

1 Tbsp ground cumin

1 Tbsp smoked paprika

1 tsp ground coriander

1 tsp garlic powder

1/2 tsp ground cinnamon

Salt and pepper, to taste

DIRECTIONS

- Mix olive oil with all spices in a bowl. Rub the mixture all over the lamb ribs. Let marinate for at least 2 hours or overnight.
- Preheat the air fryer to 375°F (190°C).
- Place the lamb ribs in the air fryer basket. Cook for 20 minutes, turning halfway through.
- Serve hot with a side of roasted vegetables or a fresh salad.

Per serving: calories 520; fat 40g; protein 35g; carbs 5g; fiber 1g

GREEK-STYLE PORK CHOPS

INGREDIENTS

4 pork chops, about 1-inch thick

2 Tbsp olive oil

Juice of 1 lemon

3 cloves garlic, minced

1 Tbsp dried oregano

1 tsp dried thyme

Salt and pepper, to taste

1/2 cup feta cheese, crumbled

Fresh parsley, chopped (for garnish)

DIRECTIONS

- Mix olive oil with all spices in a bowl.
- Marinate the pork chops in this mixture for at least 1 hour, preferably longer.
- Preheat the air fryer to 380°F (193°C).
- Place marinated pork chops in the air fryer basket. Cook for 12 minutes, flipping halfway through, or until the internal temperature reaches 145°F (63°C).
- Serve hot, topped with crumbled feta cheese, and garnished with fresh parsley.

Per serving: calories 320; fat 20g; protein 29g; carbs 2g; fiber 0g

ITALIAN HERB PORK TENDERLOIN

SERVES 4 | PREP 10 MIN | COOK 20 MIN

INGREDIENTS

1 pork tenderloin (about 1 to 1.5 pounds)

2 Tbsp olive oil

2 cloves garlic, minced

1 Tbsp dried Italian herbs (a blend of basil, oregano, rosemary, and thyme)

1 tsp salt

1/2 tsp black pepper

Fresh parsley, chopped (for garnish)

DIRECTIONS

- Mix olive oil with all spices in a bowl.
- Rub this mixture all over the pork tenderloin.
- Marinate the pork for at least 30 mins.
- Preheat the air fryer to 400°F (200°C).
- Place the pork tenderloin in the air fryer basket and cook for 20 minutes, or until the internal temperature reaches 145°F (63°C), turning halfway through cooking.
- Let the pork rest for a few minutes after cooking, then slice and garnish with fresh parsley.

Per serving: calories 220; fat 10g; protein 30g; carbs 1g; fiber 0g

SMOKY PAPRIKA PORK KEBABS

SERVES 4 | PREP 15 MIN+Marinating | COOK 10 MIN

INGREDIENTS

1 lb pork loin, cut into 1-inch cubes

2 Tbsp olive oil

2 Tbsp smoked paprika

1 tsp garlic powder

1 tsp onion powder

1/2 tsp cayenne pepper (optional)

Salt and pepper, to taste

1 red bell pepper, cut into 1-inch pieces

1 yellow bell pepper, cut into 1-inch pieces

1 onion, cut into chunks

Fresh parsley, chopped (for garnish)

DIRECTIONS

- Mix olive oil with all spices in a bowl. Add pork cubes to the bowl and marinate for at least 30 mins.
- Preheat the air fryer to 400°F (200°C).
- Thread the marinated pork and pieces of bell peppers and onion alternately onto skewers.
- Place the skewers in the air fryer basket and cook for 10 minutes, turning halfway through, until the pork is cooked through and vegetables are lightly charred.
- Garnish with fresh parsley.

Per serving: calories 250; fat 12g; protein 25g; carbs 10g; fiber 3g

VEGETABLES

Tips from the Author

"Start with lower temperatures and shorter cooking times to achieve perfectly crispy vegetables like kale chips. Adjust as needed to avoid burning and bring out the best flavors in your veggies."

MEDITERRANEAN VEGGIE NUGGETS

SERVES 4 | PREP 20 MIN | COOK 15 MIN

INGREDIENTS

1 cup cooked chickpeas, mashed

1/2 cup carrots, grated

1/2 cup zucchini, grated and squeezed

1/4 cup red bell pepper, chopped

2 cloves garlic, minced

1/4 cup parsley, chopped

2 tbsp basil, chopped

Salt and pepper

1/2 cup breadcrumbs (more for coating)

2 tbsp olive oil

Spicy Vegan Mayo:

1/2 cup vegan mayonnaise

1 tbsp Sriracha

1 tsp lemon juice

DIRECTIONS

- Combine chickpeas, vegetables, garlic, herbs, breadcrumbs, salt, and pepper.
- Shape into nuggets and coat with more breadcrumbs.
- Air fry at 375°F (190°C) for 15 minutes, flipping once.
- Mix mayo, Sriracha, and lemon juice for sauce.
- Serve nuggets with spicy mayo.

Per serving: calories 200; fat 11g; protein 6g; carbs 22g; fiber 5g

STUFFED TOMATOES

SERVES 4 | PREP 15 MIN | COOK 10 MIN

INGREDIENTS

4 large tomatoes

1 cup couscous, cooked

1/4 cup pine nuts, toasted

1/4 cup fresh parsley, chopped

1/4 cup fresh basil, chopped

2 cloves garlic, minced

2 Tbsp olive oil

Salt and pepper, to taste

1/4 cup feta cheese, crumbled (optional)

DIRECTIONS

- Slice the tops off the tomatoes and carefully scoop out the insides, leaving a sturdy shell.
- Mix couscous, pine nuts, herbs, garlic, oil, salt, and pepper; fill tomatoes with that mixture. Add feta on top.
- Air fry at 360°F (182°C) for 10 minutes until tomatoes soften.
- Serve warm, garnished with herbs.

Per serving: calories 260; fat 12g; protein 6g; carbs 34g; fiber 4g

ARTICHOKE AND SPINACH DIP

SERVES 4 | PREP 10 MIN | COOK 5 MIN

INGREDIENTS

1 can (14 oz) artichoke hearts, drained and chopped

1 cup fresh spinach, chopped

1 cup vegan cream cheese

1/2 cup vegan sour cream

1/4 cup nutritional yeast (for a cheesy flavor)

2 cloves garlic, minced

Salt and pepper, to taste

Olive oil spray

DIRECTIONS

- In a mixing bowl, combine chopped artichokes, spinach, vegan cream cheese, vegan sour cream, nutritional yeast, garlic, salt, and pepper. Mix until well blended.
- Transfer the mixture to an oven-safe dish suitable for use in an air fryer.
- Spray lightly with olive oil.
- Air fry at 360°F (182°C) for 5 minutes or until hot and bubbly.
- Serve warm with air-fried pita chips for dipping.

Per serving: calories 250; fat 18g; protein 5g; carbs 15g; fiber 4g

AIR-FRIED DOLMAS

SERVES 4 | PREP 30 MIN | COOK 10 MIN

INGREDIENTS

1 jar of grape leaves, rinsed and drained

1 cup cooked rice

1/4 cup fresh dill, chopped

1/4 cup fresh mint, chopped

1 onion, finely chopped

2 cloves garlic, minced

1/4 cup pine nuts

1 lemon, juiced

2 Tbsp olive oil

Salt and pepper, to taste

DIRECTIONS

- Combine rice, dill, mint, onion, garlic, pine nuts, lemon juice (half), olive oil, salt, and pepper.
- Stuff each grape leaf with the filling and roll tightly.
- Arrange in air fryer, seam down. Drizzle with remaining lemon juice and oil.
- Air fry at 350°F (175°C) for 10 minutes until crisp.
- Serve warm or at room temperature.

Per serving: calories 200; fat 10g; protein 4g; carbs 28g; fiber 4g

GREEK STUFFED MUSHROOMS

SERVES 4 | PREP 15 MIN | COOK 10 MIN

INGREDIENTS

12 large mushrooms, stems removed

1 cup fresh spinach, chopped

1/2 cup Kalamata olives, chopped

1/2 cup vegan feta cheese, crumbled

2 cloves garlic, minced

1 tbsp olive oil

Salt and pepper, to taste

Fresh dill or parsley for garnish

DIRECTIONS

- Combine spinach, olives, vegan feta, garlic, olive oil, salt, and pepper in a bowl.
- Stuff mushrooms with the mixture.
- Preheat air fryer to 350°F (177°C).
- Air fry stuffed mushrooms for 10 minutes.
- Garnish with dill or parsley.

Per serving: calories 150; fat 9g; protein 4g; carbs 10g; fiber 3g

ZUCCHINI AND CORN FRITTERS

SERVES 4 | PREP 15 MIN | COOK 10 MIN

INGREDIENTS

2 medium zucchinis, grated

1 cup sweet corn (fresh or thawed if frozen)

1/2 cup all-purpose flour

1 egg, beaten

2 green onions, finely chopped

1 tsp garlic powder

Salt and pepper, to taste

Olive oil spray

DIRECTIONS

- Squeeze zucchini to remove excess moisture.
- Combine zucchini, corn, flour, egg, green onions, garlic powder, salt, and pepper.
- Form into patties.
- Spray air fryer basket with oil, preheat to 375°F (190°C).
- Cook patties for 10 minutes, flipping once, until golden.
- Serve warm.

Per serving: calories 180; fat 4g; protein 6g; carbs 30g; fiber 3g

CRISPY BRUSSEL SPROUTS WITH BALSAMIC GLAZE

SERVES 4 | PREP 10 MIN | COOK 15 MIN

INGREDIENTS

1 lb Brussels sprouts, trimmed and halved

2 Tbsp olive oil

2 cloves garlic, minced

Salt and pepper, to taste

1/4 cup balsamic vinegar

1 Tbsp honey

DIRECTIONS

- Toss Brussels sprouts with olive oil, garlic, salt, and pepper.
- Air fry at 400°F (200°C) for 15 minutes, shaking halfway.
- Simmer balsamic vinegar and honey until thickened to make glaze.
- Drizzle balsamic glaze over Brussels sprouts and serve.

Per serving: calories 140; fat 7g; protein 3g; carbs 16g; fiber 4g

EGGPLANT PARMESAN

SERVES 4 | PREP 20 MIN | COOK 20 MIN

INGREDIENTS

2 medium eggplants, sliced into 1/2-inch rounds

1 cup vegan breadcrumbs

1/2 cup all-purpose flour

1 cup unsweetened almond milk

1 tsp garlic powder

1 tsp Italian seasoning

Salt and pepper, to taste

2 cups marinara sauce

1 cup vegan mozzarella cheese, shredded

DIRECTIONS

- Set up a breading station with three plates: one for flour, one for almond milk, and one for breadcrumbs mixed with garlic powder, Italian seasoning, salt, and pepper.
- Dip each eggplant slice first in flour, then almond milk, and finally coat with the breadcrumb mixture.
- Preheat the air fryer to 375°F (190°C) and spray the basket with olive oil.
- Air fry eggplant slices in batches for 10 minutes each, flipping halfway through, until golden and crispy.
- In an oven-safe dish, layer the air-fried eggplant with marinara sauce and vegan mozzarella cheese. Repeat layers until all ingredients are used.
- Air fry at 375°F (190°C) for another 10 minutes or until the cheese is melted and bubbly.
- Garnish with fresh basil and serve warm.

Per serving: calories 350; fat 12g; protein 10g; carbs 50g; fiber 8g

CAULIFLOWER STEAKS WITH TAHINI SAUCE

SERVES 4 | PREP 10 MIN | COOK 20 MIN

INGREDIENTS

1 large head of cauliflower

2 Tbsp olive oil

1 tsp smoked paprika

Salt and pepper, to taste

For the Tahini Sauce:

    1/4 cup tahini

    1 lemon, juiced

    1 clove garlic, minced

    2-4 Tbsp warm water
    (to thin)

    Salt, to taste

DIRECTIONS

- Slice cauliflower into 1-inch steaks. Brush with oil and season with paprika, salt, and pepper.
- Air fry at 400°F (200°C) for 20 minutes, flipping once.
- Mix tahini, lemon juice, garlic, and salt. Adjust consistency with warm water.
- Drizzle sauce over cauliflower steaks and serve.

Per serving: calories 210; fat 15g; protein 6g; carbs 18g;

SWEET POTATO AND CHICKPEA PATTIES

SERVES 4 | PREP 20 MIN | COOK 15 MIN

INGREDIENTS

2 large sweet potatoes, peeled and cooked until tender

1 cup chickpeas, drained and rinsed

1 onion, finely chopped

2 cloves garlic, minced

1 tsp ground cumin

1 tsp smoked paprika

1/2 tsp chili powder

Salt and pepper, to taste

2 Tbsp fresh cilantro, chopped

1/4 cup flour (optional for binding)

Olive oil spray

DIRECTIONS

- Mash sweet potatoes and chickpeas in a bowl; leave chunky.
- Mix in onion, garlic, spices, cilantro, and flour if needed.
- Shape into patties.
- Preheat air fryer to 375°F (190°C), spray basket.
- Cook patties for 15 mins; flip halfway.
- Serve warm.

Per serving: calories 210; fat 3g; protein 7g; carbs 40g; fiber 7g

VEGAN SPANAKOPITA

SERVES 4 | PREP 10 MIN | COOK 15 MIN

INGREDIENTS

8 sheets of vegan phyllo dough, thawed

2 cups fresh spinach, chopped

1 cup vegan feta cheese, crumbled

1 onion, finely chopped

2 cloves garlic, minced

2 Tbsp olive oil, plus extra for brushing

Salt and pepper, to taste

1 tsp dried dill or fresh dill, chopped

DIRECTIONS

- Sauté onion and garlic in olive oil until translucent. Add spinach and cook until wilted. Season with salt, pepper, and dill. Let the mixture cool, then stir in vegan feta.
- Carefully lay out one sheet of phyllo dough and brush lightly with olive oil. Place another sheet on top and brush again. Repeat until you have four layers.
- Place a quarter of the spinach and feta mixture on the edge of the phyllo stack and roll up tightly into a log. Tuck in the ends to seal. Repeat with remaining phyllo sheets and filling.
- Preheat the air fryer to 350°F (175°C). Brush the spanakopita rolls with olive oil and place them in the air fryer basket.
- Cook for 15 minutes, turning halfway through, until golden and crispy.

Per serving: calories 280; fat 18g; protein 5g; carbs 25g; fiber 3g

SPICED CARROT FRIES

SERVES 4 | PREP 10 MIN | COOK 20 MIN

INGREDIENTS

1 lb carrots, peeled and cut into fry-shaped sticks

2 tbsp harissa paste

1 tbsp olive oil

Salt, to taste

DIRECTIONS

- Toss carrots with harissa, olive oil, and salt.
- Preheat air fryer to 380°F (193°C).
- Arrange carrots in a single layer in the basket; air fry for 20 minutes, shaking halfway.
- Serve hot.

Per serving: calories 90; fat 3.5g; protein 1g; carbs 14g; fiber 3g

RATATOUILLE BASKETS

SERVES 4 | PREP 15 MIN | COOK 20 MIN

INGREDIENTS

4 bell peppers, halved and seeded
1 small zucchini, finely diced
1 small eggplant, finely diced
1 small yellow squash, finely diced
1 medium onion, finely diced
2 cloves garlic, minced
2 tomatoes, finely diced
1 tbsp olive oil
1 tsp dried thyme
1 tsp dried basil
Salt and pepper, to taste
Fresh parsley, chopped (for garnish)

DIRECTIONS

- In a bowl, combine zucchini, eggplant, yellow squash, onion, garlic, and tomatoes. Toss with olive oil, thyme, basil, salt, and pepper.
- Fill each bell pepper half with the vegetable mixture.
- Preheat the air fryer to 375°F (190°C).
- Place the stuffed bell peppers in the air fryer basket and cook for 20 minutes, or until the peppers are tender and the filling is cooked through.
- Garnish with fresh parsley before serving

Per serving: calories 120; fat 4g; protein 2g; carbs 20g; fiber 5g

CRISPY CHICKPEA FALAFEL

SERVES 4 | PREP 15 MIN | COOK 15 MIN

INGREDIENTS

1 cup dried chickpeas, soaked overnight
1 small onion, roughly chopped
2 cloves garlic, minced
1/4 cup fresh parsley, chopped
1/4 cup fresh cilantro, chopped
1 tsp ground cumin
1 tsp ground coriander
1/2 tsp chili powder
Salt and pepper, to taste
1/4 tsp baking powder
2 Tbsp flour
Olive oil spray

DIRECTIONS

- Drain and rinse the soaked chickpeas thoroughly.
- In a food processor, combine the chickpeas, onion, garlic, parsley, cilantro, cumin, coriander, chili powder, salt, and pepper. Process until mixture is finely ground.
- Transfer to a bowl and stir in baking powder and flour to help bind the mixture. If necessary, adjust seasoning.
- Form the mixture into small balls or patties.
- Spray each falafel lightly with olive oil.
- Preheat the air fryer to 375°F (190°C).
- Place the falafel in the air fryer basket in a single layer. Cook for 15 minutes, turning halfway through, until golden and crispy.

Per serving: calories 200; fat 6g; protein 8g; carbs 30g; fiber 7g

STUFFED BELL PEPPERS

INGREDIENTS

4 large bell peppers, tops cut off and seeds removed

1 cup cooked quinoa

1/2 cup black olives, sliced

1/2 cup sun-dried tomatoes, chopped

1 onion, finely chopped

2 cloves garlic, minced

1/4 cup fresh parsley, chopped

1 tbsp olive oil

Salt and pepper, to taste

1/2 cup crumbled feta cheese (optional)

DIRECTIONS

- Sauté onion and garlic in oil until soft. Combine with quinoa, olives, sun-dried tomatoes, parsley, salt, and pepper.
- Fill peppers with the mixture.
- Air fry at 360°F (182°C) for 20 minutes. Add feta in the last 5 minutes if using.
- Serve warm

Per serving: calories 250; fat 9g; protein 6g; carbs 35g; fiber 6g

AIR-FRIED ASPARAGUS WITH ALMOND CRUMBS

INGREDIENTS

1 lb fresh asparagus, ends trimmed

1/2 cup almond meal

Zest of 1 lemon

2 tablespoons olive oil

Salt and pepper, to taste

Lemon wedges for serving

DIRECTIONS

- Coat asparagus in olive oil.
- Mix almond meal, lemon zest, salt, and pepper. Roll asparagus in this mixture.
- Preheat air fryer to 400°F (200°C).
- Air fry asparagus in a single layer for 8 mins or until golden and crisp.
- Serve with lemon wedges.

Per serving: calories 150; fat 11g; protein 5g; carbs 10g; fiber 4g

VEGAN MUSHROOM GYROS

SERVES 4 | PREP 15 MIN | COOK 10 MIN

INGREDIENTS

1 lb portobello mushrooms, thinly sliced

2 tbsp olive oil

2 cloves garlic, minced

1 tbsp smoked paprika

1 tsp ground cumin

1 tsp dried oregano

1 tsp ground coriander

Salt and pepper, to taste

4 pita breads

Vegan tzatziki

Sliced tomatoes, onions, and lettuce for serving

DIRECTIONS

- Mix olive oil, garlic, and spices in a bowl; marinate mushrooms for 30 minutes.
- Air fry at 375°F (190°C) for 10 minutes, stir halfway.
- Warm pitas; fill with mushrooms, tzatziki, tomatoes, onions, and lettuce.
- Serve immediately.

Per serving: calories 300; fat 12g; protein 8g; carbs 40g; fiber 6g

GARLIC LEMON BROCCOLI

SERVES 4 | PREP 5 MIN | COOK 10 MIN

INGREDIENTS

1 lb broccoli florets

2 tbsp olive oil

3 cloves garlic, minced

Salt and pepper, to taste

Juice of 1 lemon

DIRECTIONS

- Toss broccoli florets with olive oil, minced garlic, salt, and pepper in a bowl.
- Preheat the air fryer to 375°F (190°C).
- Spread the broccoli evenly in the air fryer basket.
- Cook for 10 minutes, shaking the basket halfway through.
- Once cooked, drizzle fresh lemon juice over the broccoli and serve immediately.

Per serving: calories 90; fat 7g; protein 3g; carbs 6g; fiber 2g

VEGAN POTATO CROQUETTES

SERVES 4 | PREP 20 MIN | COOK 15 MIN

INGREDIENTS

2 cups mashed potatoes (cooled)

1/2 cup carrots, finely chopped

1/2 cup peas

1/4 cup green onions, finely chopped

1/4 cup nutritional yeast (for a cheesy flavor)

1 tsp garlic powder

Salt and pepper, to taste

1/2 cup flour (for coating)

1/2 cup unsweetened almond milk

1 cup breadcrumbs

Olive oil spray

DIRECTIONS

- Combine potatoes, carrots, peas, green onions, nutritional yeast, garlic powder, salt, and pepper.
- Shape into croquettes.
- Dredge in flour, dip in almond milk, then coat with breadcrumbs.
- Preheat air fryer to 400°F (200°C).
- Spray basket with oil, add croquettes, and cook for 15 minutes, turning once.
- Serve hot.

Per serving: calories 220; fat 4g; protein 6g; carbs 40g; fiber 5g

BUTTERNUT SQUASH CHIPS

SERVES 4 | PREP 10 MIN | COOK 20 MIN

INGREDIENTS

1 medium butternut squash

1 tbsp olive oil

Salt, to taste

Optional seasonings: paprika, garlic powder, black pepper

DIRECTIONS

- Peel and thinly slice the butternut squash.
- Toss slices with olive oil and seasonings.
- Preheat air fryer to 375°F (190°C).
- Air fry in batches, single layer, for 20 minutes, flipping halfway.
- Serve immediately.

Per serving: calories 80; fat 3.5g; protein 1g; carbs 12g; fiber 2g

SIDES & SALADS

Tips from the Author

"Add a crispy element to your salads by air frying ingredients like chickpeas or croutons. The air fryer brings a satisfying crunch without the extra oil, making your sides and salads even more enjoyable."

AIR-FRIED GARLIC PARMESAN ZUCCHINI

SERVES 4 | PREP 10 MIN | COOK 15 MIN

INGREDIENTS

2 large zucchini, sliced into 1/4-inch rounds

3 Tbsp olive oil

2 cloves garlic, minced

1/2 cup Parmesan cheese, grated

1/4 tsp salt

1/4 tsp black pepper

DIRECTIONS

- In a large bowl, toss zucchini slices with olive oil and minced garlic.
- Mix in Parmesan cheese, salt, and pepper until zucchini slices are evenly coated.
- Place zucchini in a single layer in the air fryer basket. Air fry at 400°F for about 15 mins or until crispy and golden.

Per serving: calories 150; fat 11g; protein 6g; carbs 8g; fiber 2g.

MEDITERRANEAN ROASTED BELL PEPPERS

SERVES 4 | PREP 10 MIN | COOK 15 MIN

INGREDIENTS

4 large bell peppers (red, yellow, green, and orange), sliced

3 Tbsp olive oil

3 cloves garlic, minced

1 tsp dried oregano

1 tsp dried basil

1/2 tsp salt

1/4 tsp black pepper

DIRECTIONS

- In a large bowl, combine bell pepper slices, olive oil, minced garlic, oregano, basil, salt, and pepper. Toss to coat evenly.
- Arrange the seasoned bell peppers in a single layer in the air fryer basket.
- Air fry at 400°F for about 15 minutes, stirring halfway through, until the peppers are tender and slightly charred.

Per serving: calories 120; fat 10g; protein 1g; carbs 8g; fiber 2g.

GREEK SALAD WITH AIR-FRIED PITA CHIPS

SERVES 4 | PREP 15 MIN | COOK 10 MIN

INGREDIENTS

3 medium tomatoes, chopped

1 cucumber, peeled and diced

1 red onion, thinly sliced

1/2 cup Kalamata olives, pitted

1/2 cup feta cheese, crumbled

1/4 cup olive oil

2 Tbsp red wine vinegar

1 tsp dried oregano

Salt and pepper to taste

4 pita breads, cut into triangles

DIRECTIONS

- In a large bowl, combine tomatoes, cucumber, red onion, olives, and feta cheese.
- Drizzle with olive oil and red wine vinegar. Add oregano, salt, and pepper.
- Arrange pita triangles in a single layer in the air fryer basket. Air fry at 360°F for about 10 minutes or until crispy and golden.
- Serve the salad topped with air-fried pita chips for added crunch.

Per serving: calories 340; fat 21g; protein 8g; carbs 32g; fiber 5g.

COUSCOUS TABBOULEH

SERVES 4 | PREP 15 MIN | COOK 5 MIN

INGREDIENTS

1 cup couscous, cooked

1 cup parsley, finely chopped

1/2 cup mint leaves, finely chopped

2 medium tomatoes, diced

1 cucumber, diced

4 green onions, sliced

1/4 cup lemon juice

1/4 cup olive oil

1 tsp salt

1/2 tsp black pepper

DIRECTIONS

- In a large bowl, combine cooked couscous with parsley, mint, tomatoes, cucumber, and green onions.
- In a small bowl, whisk together lemon juice, olive oil, salt, and pepper.
- Pour the dressing over the couscous mixture and toss to combine thoroughly.
- Chill in the refrigerator before serving to allow the flavors to meld.

Per serving: calories 260; fat 14g; protein 6g; carbs 31g; fiber 5g.

AIR-FRIED ARTICHOKES WITH LEMON DIPPING SAUCE

INGREDIENTS

- 4 whole artichokes, trimmed and halved
- 2 Tbsp olive oil
- 1 tsp salt
- 1/2 tsp black pepper
-
- **For the Lemon Dipping Sauce:**
- 1/4 cup mayonnaise
- 2 Tbsp lemon juice
- 1 clove garlic, minced
- 1 tsp Dijon mustard
- Salt and pepper to taste

DIRECTIONS

- Brush the artichoke halves with olive oil and season with salt and pepper.
- Place the artichoke halves in the air fryer basket, cut side down. Air fry at 375°F for about 15 minutes.
- For the lemon dipping sauce, combine mayonnaise, lemon juice, minced garlic, and Dijon mustard in a small bowl. Season with salt and pepper to taste and whisk until smooth.
- Serve the artichokes hot with the lemon dipping sauce on the side.

Per serving: calories 220; fat 17g; protein 3g; carbs 16g; fiber 7g.

SPICED CHICKPEA SALAD

INGREDIENTS

2 cups chickpeas, cooked and drained

1/4 cup olive oil

1 tsp cumin

1 tsp paprika

1/4 cup fresh parsley, chopped

1/4 cup fresh cilantro, chopped

2 Tbsp fresh mint, chopped

1 medium red onion, chopped

2 Tbsp lemon juice

Salt and pepper to taste

DIRECTIONS

- In a large bowl, combine chickpeas, olive oil, cumin, paprika, parsley, cilantro, mint, and red onion.
- Drizzle with lemon juice and season with salt and pepper. Toss well to combine.
- Serve the salad cold or at room temperature to allow the flavors to meld together.

Per serving: calories 250; fat 14g; protein 7g; carbs 27g; fiber 6g.

FATTOUSH WITH AIR-FRIED BREAD

SERVES 4 | PREP 20 MIN | COOK 5 MIN

INGREDIENTS

3 cups romaine lettuce, chopped

1 cup cucumbers, diced

1 cup tomatoes, chopped

1/2 cup radishes, sliced

1/4 cup green onions, sliced

1/4 cup fresh mint leaves, chopped

1/4 cup fresh parsley, chopped

2 pita breads, cut into squares

3 Tbsp olive oil

2 Tbsp lemon juice

1 tsp sumac

1/2 tsp salt

1/4 tsp black pepper

DIRECTIONS

- Toss pita strips with 1 Tbsp olive oil and air fry at 350°F until crispy, about 5 minutes.
- Mix lettuce, cucumbers, tomatoes, radishes, onions, mint, and parsley in a large bowl.
- Whisk together 2 Tbsp olive oil, lemon juice, sumac, salt, and pepper for the dressing.
- Toss salad with dressing and top with crispy pita just before serving.

Per serving: calories 220; fat 10g; protein 4g; carbs 29g; fiber 5g

BABA GHANOUSH WITH AIR-FRIED EGGPLANT

SERVES 4 | PREP 10 MIN | COOK 15 MIN

INGREDIENTS

2 large eggplants

3 Tbsp olive oil

2 cloves garlic, minced

2 Tbsp tahini

2 Tbsp lemon juice

1/2 tsp salt

1/4 tsp ground cumin

Paprika and fresh parsley for garnish

DIRECTIONS

- Halve the eggplants lengthwise and brush with 1 tablespoon of olive oil. Air fry at 400°F until soft and the skin is slightly charred about 15 minutes.
- Scoop the eggplant flesh into a bowl, discarding the skin.
- Add garlic, tahini, remaining olive oil, lemon juice, salt, and cumin. Blend until smooth.
- Garnish with paprika and parsley. Serve with vegetable sticks or flatbread.

Per serving: calories 180; fat 11g; protein 3g; carbs 20g; fiber 6g

LEMON AND HERB POTATOES

SERVES 4 | PREP 10 MIN | COOK 20 MIN

INGREDIENTS

1.5 lbs baby potatoes, halved

3 Tbsp olive oil

Zest of 1 lemon

2 cloves garlic, minced

1 tsp dried rosemary

1 tsp dried thyme

1/2 tsp salt

1/4 tsp black pepper

DIRECTIONS

- Toss potatoes with olive oil, lemon zest, garlic, rosemary, thyme, salt, and pepper.
- Air fry at 400°F for 20 minutes, shaking the basket halfway through, until golden and crispy.

Per serving: calories 220; fat 10g; protein 4g; carbs 30g; fiber 4g.

AIR-FRIED STUFFED GRAPE LEAVES

SERVES 4 | PREP 30 MIN | COOK 15 MIN

INGREDIENTS

30 grape leaves, rinsed and patted dry

1 cup cooked rice

1/4 cup fresh dill, chopped

1/4 cup fresh parsley, chopped

1 Tbsp fresh mint, chopped

2 Tbsp olive oil

Zest and juice of 1 lemon

1 tsp salt

1/2 tsp black pepper

DIRECTIONS

- In a mixing bowl, combine rice, dill, parsley, mint, olive oil, lemon zest, lemon juice, salt, and pepper.
- Place a tablespoon of the filling in the center of each grape leaf. Fold sides over the filling and roll tightly.
- Arrange the stuffed grape leaves in a single layer in the air fryer basket.
- Air fry at 360°F for about 15 minutes, turning halfway through, until the leaves are crispy and golden.

Per serving: calories 150; fat 7g; protein 3g; carbs 20g; fiber 3g.

CUCUMBER AND YOGURT SALAD

SERVES 4 | PREP 10 MIN | COOK 0 MIN

INGREDIENTS

2 large cucumbers, peeled and diced

2 cups plain Greek yogurt

2 cloves garlic, minced

2 Tbsp fresh mint, finely chopped

1 Tbsp olive oil

1/2 tsp salt

A pinch of black pepper

Fresh dill or mint for garnish

DIRECTIONS

- Combine cucumbers, Greek yogurt, garlic, mint, olive oil, salt, and pepper in a bowl.
- Mix well until all ingredients are fully incorporated.
- Chill in the refrigerator for at least 30 minutes before serving to enhance the flavors.
- Garnish with fresh dill or mint before serving.

Per serving: calories 130; fat 6g; protein 10g; carbs 10g; fiber 2g.

MEDITERRANEAN BEAN SALAD

SERVES 4 | PREP 15 MIN | COOK 0 MIN

INGREDIENTS

1 can (15 oz) of each: chickpeas, kidney beans, black beans

1 red bell pepper

1 yellow bell pepper

1 red onion

1/4 cup olive oil

3 Tbsp red wine vinegar

1 tsp dried oregano

1/2 tsp salt

1/4 tsp black pepper

Fresh parsley, chopped for garnish

DIRECTIONS

- Drain and rinse all canned beans.
- In a large bowl, combine chickpeas, kidney beans, black beans, diced red bell pepper, yellow bell pepper, and chopped red onion.
- In a small bowl, whisk together olive oil, red wine vinegar, oregano, salt, and pepper.
- Pour the vinaigrette over the bean mixture and toss to coat evenly.
- Chill in the refrigerator for at least an hour before serving.
- Garnish with fresh parsley.

Per serving: calories 320; fat 10g; protein 15g; carbs 45g; fiber 12g.

CAPRESE SALAD WITH BALSAMIC REDUCTION

SERVES 4 | PREP 10 MIN | COOK 10 MIN

INGREDIENTS

4 large ripe tomatoes, sliced

8 oz fresh mozzarella cheese, sliced

1/4 cup fresh basil leaves

1/2 cup balsamic vinegar

2 Tbsp honey

1/4 cup olive oil

Salt and pepper to taste

DIRECTIONS

- Alternate tomato and mozzarella slices on a plate; add basil.
- Simmer balsamic vinegar and honey until reduced by half, about 10 minutes; cool.
- Drizzle with olive oil and balsamic reduction.
- Season with salt and pepper.

Per serving: calories 280; fat 20g; protein 12g; carbs 16g; fiber 2g.

ROASTED BEET AND FETA SALAD

SERVES 4 | PREP 10 MIN | COOK 6 MIN

INGREDIENTS

4 medium beets, peeled and diced

1/4 cup walnuts, chopped

1/2 cup feta cheese, crumbled

1/4 cup olive oil

2 Tbsp red wine vinegar

1 tsp honey

1/2 tsp salt

1/4 tsp black pepper

Fresh parsley, chopped for garnish

DIRECTIONS

- Roast beets at 400°F in air fryer until tender, about 30 minutes.
- Whisk olive oil, vinegar, honey, salt, and pepper for dressing.
- Toss beets, walnuts, and feta with dressing.
- Garnish with parsley.

Per serving: calories 250; fat 19g; protein 6g; carbs 17g; fiber 4g.

AIR-FRIED ASPARAGUS WITH ALMONDS

SERVES 4 | PREP 5 MIN | COOK 10 MIN

INGREDIENTS

1 lb asparagus, ends trimmed

2 Tbsp olive oil

1/4 cup slivered almonds

Salt and pepper to taste

DIRECTIONS

- Toss asparagus with olive oil, salt, and pepper.
- Air fry at 400°F for 7 minutes.
- Add almonds and air fry for another 3 minutes, until asparagus is tender and almonds are toasted.

Per serving: calories 120; fat 9g; protein 4g; carbs 7g; fiber 3g.

QUINOA SALAD WITH DRIED FRUITS AND NUTS

SERVES 4 | PREP 10 MIN | COOK 15 MIN

INGREDIENTS

1 cup quinoa, rinsed

2 cups water

1/4 cup dried apricots, chopped

1/4 cup raisins

1/4 cup almonds, chopped

1/4 cup fresh parsley, chopped

3 Tbsp olive oil

2 Tbsp lemon juice

1 tsp honey

Salt and pepper to taste

DIRECTIONS

- Cook quinoa in water according to package instructions until fluffy.
- In a large bowl, combine cooked quinoa, apricots, raisins, almonds, and parsley.
- Whisk olive oil, lemon juice, honey, salt, and pepper to make the dressing.
- Pour dressing over salad and toss to combine.

Per serving: calories 320; fat 15g; protein 8g; carbs 42g; fiber 5g.

ORZO WITH SPINACH AND PINE NUTS

SERVES 4 | PREP 10 MIN | COOK 10 MIN

INGREDIENTS

1 cup orzo pasta

2 cups fresh spinach, roughly chopped

1/4 cup pine nuts, toasted

1/2 cup feta cheese, crumbled

2 Tbsp olive oil

Salt and pepper to taste

DIRECTIONS

- Cook orzo according to package instructions until al dente; drain.
- In a large skillet, sauté spinach in olive oil until wilted, about 2 minutes.
- Toss cooked orzo with sautéed spinach, pine nuts, and feta cheese.
- Season with salt and pepper to taste.

Per serving: calories 280; fat 12g; protein 10g; carbs 34g; fiber 3g.

AIR-FRIED BRUSSELS SPROUTS WITH POMEGRANATE MOLASSES

SERVES 4 | PREP 10 MIN | COOK 15 MIN

INGREDIENTS

1 lb Brussels sprouts, trimmed and halved

2 Tbsp olive oil

Salt and pepper to taste

2 Tbsp pomegranate molasses

Optional garnish: pomegranate seeds and chopped parsley

DIRECTIONS

- Toss Brussels sprouts with olive oil, salt, and pepper.
- Air fry at 375°F for about 15 minutes, shaking the basket halfway through, until crispy and golden.
- Drizzle with pomegranate molasses before serving.
- Garnish with pomegranate seeds and parsley if desired.

Per serving: calories 160; fat 7g; protein 4g; carbs 23g; fiber 5g.

MARINATED OLIVES AND FETA

SERVES 4 | PREP 10 MIN | COOK 0 MIN

INGREDIENTS

1 cup mixed olives

1 cup feta cheese, cubed

1/4 cup olive oil

2 cloves garlic, minced

1 tsp dried oregano

1 tsp dried rosemary

Zest of 1 lemon

Black pepper to taste

DIRECTIONS

- In a bowl, combine olives, feta cheese, olive oil, garlic, oregano, rosemary, lemon zest, and black pepper.
- Mix well to coat all ingredients evenly.
- Let marinate for at least 30 minutes, preferably longer, in the refrigerator to enhance the flavors.

Per serving: calories 250; fat 23g; protein 7g; carbs 4g; fiber 1g.

CHARRED CORN SALAD WITH MINT AND FETA

SERVES 4 | PREP 10 MIN | COOK 10 MIN

INGREDIENTS

4 cups corn kernels

1/4 cup feta cheese

1/4 cup fresh mint leaves

2 Tbsp olive oil

Juice of 1 lime

Salt and pepper to taste

DIRECTIONS

- Toss corn with 1 tablespoon of olive oil
- Air fry at 400°F for about 10 minutes, shaking occasionally, until corn is charred and crispy.
- Transfer the charred corn to a salad bowl and let cool slightly.
- Add feta cheese, mint, lime juice, and remaining olive oil to the corn. Season with salt and pepper.
- Toss everything together until well combined.

Per serving: calories 200; fat 9g; protein 5g; carbs 28g; fiber 4g

GRAINS & LEGUMES

Tips from the Author

"Toast grains and legumes in your air fryer for added depth and texture. A quick air fry can enhance their natural flavors and make them a delightful addition to any dish. Experiment with different seasonings for a tasty twist."

AIR-FRIED BEAN AND CHEESE TAQUITOS

SERVES 4 | PREP 10 MIN | COOK 8 MIN

INGREDIENTS

8 corn tortillas

1 cup black beans, cooked and slightly mashed

1 cup shredded cheese (cheddar or a blend suitable for melting)

1 teaspoon ground cumin

Salt and pepper to taste

Optional toppings: sour cream, salsa, guacamole

DIRECTIONS

- Warm tortillas slightly to make them pliable.
- Mix black beans with cumin, salt, and pepper.
- Spoon about 2 tablespoons of the bean mixture onto each tortilla and sprinkle with cheese.
- Roll the tortillas tightly around the filling.
- Place taquitos seam-side down in the air fryer basket, making sure they don't touch.
- Air fry at 400°F for about 8 minutes, or until crispy and golden.
- Serve with optional toppings like sour cream, salsa, or guacamole.

Per serving: calories 250; fat 10g; protein 12g; carbs 30g; fiber 5g.

FARRO AND ROASTED VEGETABLE SALAD

SERVES 4 | PREP 10 MIN | COOK 20 MIN

INGREDIENTS

1 cup farro, rinsed

2 cups water

1 zucchini, sliced into half-moons

1 bell pepper, sliced

1 cup cherry tomatoes, halved

3 tablespoons olive oil, divided

2 tablespoons balsamic vinegar

1 teaspoon honey

1 teaspoon Dijon mustard

Salt and pepper to taste

Fresh basil, chopped (for garnish)

DIRECTIONS

- Cook farro in water until tender, about 30 minutes. Drain if needed.
- Toss zucchini, bell pepper, and tomatoes with 1 tablespoon olive oil and season. Air fry at 400°F for 15 minutes, stirring halfway.
- Whisk 2 tablespoons olive oil, balsamic vinegar, honey, and mustard for dressing.
- Combine farro, air-fried vegetables, and dressing. Season to taste.
- Garnish with basil.

Per serving: calories 320; fat 11g; protein 8g; carbs 48g; fiber 10g.

LEMONY LENTIL AND QUINOA SALAD

INGREDIENTS

1/2 cup quinoa

1/2 cup green lentils

2 cups water (divided for cooking quinoa and lentils)

1 cucumber, diced

1 cup cherry tomatoes, halved

1/4 cup fresh parsley

1/4 cup olive oil

DIRECTIONS

- Cook quinoa and lentils separately in 1 cup of water each until tender, about 15-20 minutes. Drain and let cool.
- Combine cooked quinoa, lentils, cucumber, cherry tomatoes, and parsley.
- Whisk olive oil, lemon juice, minced garlic, salt, and pepper to make the dressing.
- Pour the dressing over the salad and toss to combine thoroughly.
- Adjust seasoning with salt and pepper if needed.

Per serving: calories 270; fat 14g; protein 9g; carbs 30g; fiber 7g.

AIR-FRIED LENTIL FRITTERS WITH YOGURT DIP

INGREDIENTS

For the fritters:

- 2 cups cooked lentils
- 1 small onion
- 2 cloves garlic
- 1/4 cup fresh parsley
- 1 tsp ground cumin
- 1/2 tsp paprika
- Salt and pepper to taste
- 1 egg
- 1/4 cup flour
- Olive oil for brushing

For the yogurt dip:

- 1 cup Greek yogurt
- 1 small cucumber, grated
- 1 clove garlic
- 1 tbsp lemon juice
- Salt and pepper to taste

DIRECTIONS

- **Fritters:**
  - Combine mashed lentils, onion, garlic, parsley, cumin, paprika, salt, and pepper in a bowl.
  - Mix in the egg and flour until well combined.
  - Form the mixture into small patties.
  - Brush each patty lightly with olive oil and air fry at 390°F for about 15 minutes, turning halfway through, until golden and crispy.
- **Yogurt Dip:**
  - In a bowl, mix Greek yogurt, grated cucumber, minced garlic, lemon juice, salt, and pepper until combined.
- Serve the hot lentil fritters with the cool yogurt dip.

Per serving: calories 250; fat 6g; protein 14g; carbs 35g; fiber 8g

FARRO WITH CHARRED LEMON BROCCOLI

SERVES 4 | PREP 10 MIN | COOK 30 MIN

INGREDIENTS

1 cup farro, rinsed

3 cups water or vegetable broth

2 cups broccoli florets

1 lemon, thinly sliced

2 cloves garlic, minced

3 tablespoons olive oil

Salt and pepper to taste

DIRECTIONS

- Cook farro in water or broth until tender, about 25-30 minutes; drain.
- Combine broccoli, lemon slices, garlic, and 2 tablespoons olive oil; season with salt and pepper.
- Air fry at 400°F for 15 minutes, stirring halfway, until broccoli is charred.
- Mix charred broccoli with cooked farro, add remaining olive oil, and season as needed.

Per serving: calories 270; fat 11g; protein 7g; carbs 38g; fiber 9g.

AIR-FRIED BLACK BEAN TOSTADAS

SERVES 4 | PREP 15 MIN | COOK 10 MIN

INGREDIENTS

4 corn tortillas

1 can (15 oz) black beans, drained and rinsed

1 tsp ground cumin

Salt and pepper to taste

1 cup shredded lettuce

1 tomato, diced

1/2 cup shredded cheese (cheddar or Mexican blend)

Optional toppings: sour cream, sliced avocado, or salsa

DIRECTIONS

- Lightly brush tortillas with oil and air fry at 400°F for about 3-4 minutes per side, until crisp.
- Mash black beans with cumin, salt, and pepper. Air fry at 350°F for about 5 minutes to warm up.
- Spread the warm mashed beans on each crisp tortilla.
- Top with shredded lettuce, diced tomatoes, and shredded cheese.
- Return tostadas to the air fryer for about 2 minutes at 350°F, just until the cheese is melted and toppings are warmed.
- Serve with optional toppings like sour cream, avocado, or salsa.

Per serving: calories 250; fat 6g; protein 10g; carbs 40g; fiber 8g.

AIR-FRIED BUCKWHEAT AND VEGETABLE PATTIES

SERVES 4 | PREP 20 MIN | COOK 15 MIN

INGREDIENTS

1 cup buckwheat groats

2 cups water

1 small carrot, grated

1 zucchini, grated

1 small onion, finely chopped

2 cloves garlic, minced

1/2 cup breadcrumbs

1 egg, beaten

1 tsp salt

1/2 tsp black pepper

1/2 tsp paprika

Olive oil for brushing

DIRECTIONS

- Cook buckwheat in water until tender; drain and let cool.
- Mix buckwheat with carrot, zucchini, onion, garlic, breadcrumbs, egg, salt, pepper, and paprika.
- Form into palm-sized patties; brush with oil.
- Air fry at 360°F for 15 minutes, flipping once, until golden and crispy.
- Serve hot with your choice of dip.

Per serving: calories 220; fat 4g; protein 7g; carbs 40g; fiber 6g.

FARRO AND AIR-FRIED VEGGIE SALAD

SERVES 4 | PREP 15 MIN | COOK 20 MIN

INGREDIENTS

1 cup farro, rinsed

3 cups water

1 zucchini, sliced into half-moons

1 red bell pepper, chopped

1 yellow bell pepper, chopped

1 carrot, sliced

1 red onion, sliced

2 tablespoons olive oil for veggies

For the dressing:

1/4 cup olive oil

2 tablespoons balsamic vinegar

1 teaspoon Dijon mustard

1 clove garlic, minced

Salt and pepper to taste

DIRECTIONS

- Cook farro in water until tender; drain and cool.
- Toss zucchini, bell peppers, carrot, and onion with olive oil, salt, and pepper. Air fry at 400°F for 15-20 minutes until charred, shaking halfway.
- Whisk olive oil, balsamic vinegar, mustard, garlic, salt, and pepper for dressing.
- Mix farro, air-fried veggies, and dressing in a large bowl. Adjust seasoning.

Per serving: calories 320; fat 14g; protein 7g; carbs 45g; fiber 8g.

BUCKWHEAT AND ROASTED VEGETABLE BOWL

SERVES 4 | PREP 15 MIN | COOK 25 MIN

INGREDIENTS

1 cup buckwheat groats

2 cups water

1 zucchini, chopped

1 red bell pepper, chopped

1 yellow bell pepper, chopped

1 red onion, chopped

1 sweet potato, peeled and diced

2 tablespoons olive oil

Salt and pepper to taste

For the dressing:

3 tablespoons olive oil

2 tablespoons apple cider vinegar

1 teaspoon honey

1 teaspoon Dijon mustard

Fresh parsley or cilantro, chopped (for garnish)

DIRECTIONS

- Cook buckwheat in boiling water until tender, about 10-12 minutes; drain.
- Toss vegetables with olive oil, salt, and pepper. Air fry at 400°F for 15-20 minutes until tender and charred.
- Whisk together dressing ingredients.
- Mix buckwheat and vegetables in a bowl, drizzle with dressing, and toss.
- Garnish with parsley or cilantro.

Per serving: calories 350; fat 14g; protein 6g; carbs 50g; fiber 7g.

LENTIL PATTIES WITH TZATZIKI

SERVES 4 | PREP 20 MIN | COOK 15 MIN

INGREDIENTS

For the lentil patties:

2 cups cooked lentils (brown or green)

1 small onion, finely chopped

2 cloves garlic, minced

1 tsp cumin

1/2 tsp smoked paprika

1/2 tsp salt

1/4 tsp black pepper

1 egg

1/2 cup breadcrumbs

For the tzatziki:

1 cup Greek yogurt

1 small cucumber, grated and excess water squeezed out

2 cloves garlic, minced

1 Tbsp olive oil

1 Tbsp lemon juice

1 Tbsp fresh dill, chopped

Salt and pepper to taste

DIRECTIONS

For the lentil patties:

- In a large bowl, mash the lentils slightly. Mix in onion, garlic, cumin, paprika, salt, pepper, egg, and breadcrumbs until well combined.
- Form the mixture into small patties.
- Air fry at 360°F for about 15 minutes, flipping halfway through, until golden and firm.

For the tzatziki:

- In a bowl, combine Greek yogurt, grated cucumber, garlic, olive oil, lemon juice, and dill. Season with salt and pepper to taste. Chill until ready to serve.

Per serving: calories 320; fat 8g; protein 18g; carbs 42g; fiber 9g.

CRISPY CHICKPEA AND SPINACH CAKES

SERVES 4 | PREP 15 MIN | COOK 20 MIN

INGREDIENTS

1 can (15 oz) chickpeas, drained and rinsed

2 cups fresh spinach, chopped

1 medium onion, finely chopped

2 cloves garlic, minced

1 tsp cumin

1/2 tsp coriander

1/2 tsp smoked paprika

Salt and pepper to taste

1 egg

1/2 cup breadcrumbs

DIRECTIONS

- In a food processor, pulse chickpeas, spinach, onion, garlic, cumin, coriander, paprika, salt, and pepper until combined but still slightly chunky.
- Transfer to a bowl, mix in the egg and breadcrumbs to form a thick mixture.
- Shape the mixture into small, flat cakes.
- Air fry at 375°F for about 20 minutes, flipping halfway through, until the cakes are golden and crispy.
- Serve hot with lemon wedges and a side of yogurt, if desired.

Per serving: calories 250; fat 6g; protein 12g; carbs 38g; fiber 8g.

AIR-FRIED RISOTTO BALLS

SERVES 4 | PREP 20 MIN | COOK 15 MIN

INGREDIENTS

2 cups cooked risotto, chilled

1/2 cup green peas, cooked

1/2 cup grated Parmesan cheese

2 eggs, beaten

1 cup breadcrumbs

Salt and pepper to taste

Optional: Marinara sauce for dipping

DIRECTIONS

- In a bowl, mix the chilled risotto, peas, and Parmesan cheese. Season with salt and pepper.
- Form the mixture into small balls about the size of a golf ball.
- Dip each ball first into beaten eggs, then roll in breadcrumbs to coat thoroughly.
- Place the risotto balls in the air fryer basket, ensuring they do not touch.
- Air fry at 375°F for about 15 minutes, or until the balls are golden brown and crispy, turning halfway through.
- Serve hot with marinara sauce for dipping, if desired.

Per serving: calories 330; fat 12g; protein 14g; carbs 42g; fiber 3g.

STUFFED EGGPLANTS WITH BULGUR AND PINE NUTS

SERVES 4 | PREP 20 MIN | COOK 25 MIN

INGREDIENTS

2 medium eggplants, halved lengthwise

1 cup bulgur wheat, cooked

1/4 cup pine nuts, toasted

1 onion, finely chopped

2 cloves garlic, minced

1 tsp cumin

1/2 tsp smoked paprika

1/4 cup fresh parsley, chopped

Salt and pepper to taste

Olive oil for brushing

For the lemon-tahini sauce:

1/4 cup tahini

2 Tbsp lemon juice

1 clove garlic, minced

Water to thin

Salt to taste

DIRECTIONS

- Scoop out the centers of the eggplant halves to create a shell, leaving a border around the edges. Chop the scooped-out flesh.

- In a pan, sauté the chopped eggplant, onion, and garlic with a little olive oil until softened.

- Stir in the cooked bulgur, pine nuts, cumin, paprika, and parsley. Season with salt and pepper.

- Brush the eggplant shells with olive oil and stuff them with the bulgur mixture.

- Air fry at 360°F for about 25 minutes, or until the eggplants are tender and the tops are golden.

- For the sauce, whisk together tahini, lemon juice, garlic, and enough water to reach a pourable consistency. Season with salt.

- Drizzle the lemon-tahini sauce over the cooked stuffed eggplants before serving.

Per serving: calories 300; fat 15g; protein 8g; carbs 38g; fiber 9g.

BARLEY AND MUSHROOM PILAF

SERVES 4 | PREP 10 MIN | COOK 30 MIN

INGREDIENTS

- 1 cup pearl barley
- 2 cups vegetable broth
- 1 onion, chopped
- 2 cloves garlic
- 1 cup mushrooms, sliced
- 2 tablespoons olive oil
- 1 teaspoon thyme
- Salt and pepper to taste
- Fresh parsley for garnish

DIRECTIONS

- Sauté onion and garlic in olive oil until translucent. Add mushrooms and cook until browned.
- Add barley, thyme, salt, and pepper; toast briefly.
- Pour in broth, bring to a boil, then simmer covered for 25 minutes until barley is tender.
- Transfer to air fryer basket; air fry at 360°F for 5 minutes for a crispy top.
- Garnish with parsley before serving.

Per serving: calories 250; fat 7g; protein 6g; carbs 44g; fiber 8g.

MUJADARA - LENTILS AND RICE WITH CRISPY ONIONS

SERVES 4 | PREP 25 MIN | COOK 30 MIN

INGREDIENTS

- 1 cup brown lentils, rinsed
- 1 cup rice, rinsed
- 3 cups water
- 2 large onions, thinly sliced
- 1/2 teaspoon ground cumin
- 1/2 teaspoon ground coriander
- Salt and pepper to taste
- 3 tablespoons olive oil
- Fresh parsley, chopped (for garnish)

DIRECTIONS

- Boil lentils in water for 15 minutes.
- Add rice, cumin, coriander, salt, and pepper; cover and cook for 20 minutes until tender.
- Toss onions with olive oil and salt; air fry at 370°F for 10 minutes until crispy.
- Top lentils and rice with crispy onions and garnish with parsley.

Per serving: calories 340; fat 10g; protein 12g; carbs 52g; fiber 12g.

DESSERTS

AIR-FRIED BAKLAVA BITES

SERVES 4 | PREP 20 MIN | COOK 8 MIN

INGREDIENTS

8 sheets of phyllo dough, cut into 4-inch squares

1 cup mixed nuts (walnuts, pistachios, almonds), finely chopped

1/4 cup sugar

1 tsp ground cinnamon

1/2 cup melted butter

1/2 cup honey

2 Tbsp water

1 tsp vanilla extract

Juice of 1/2 lemon

DIRECTIONS

- Mix nuts, sugar, and cinnamon.
- Layer 4 phyllo squares, brushing each with butter. Place the nut mixture in the center and fold the edges to form a parcel.
- Air fry at 350°F for 8 minutes or until golden.
- Simmer honey, water, vanilla, and lemon juice; drizzle over bites.

Per serving: calories 420; fat 24g; protein 6g; carbs 50g; fiber 2g.

FIG AND HONEY YOGURT CUPS

SERVES 4 | PREP 10 MIN | COOK 6 MIN

INGREDIENTS

8 fresh figs, halved

2 cups Greek yogurt

4 Tbsp honey

Optional: chopped nuts or mint for garnish

DIRECTIONS

- Air fry fig halves at 380°F for about 5 minutes or until juicy and slightly caramelized.
- Spoon Greek yogurt into cups, top with warm figs, drizzle with honey and garnish if desired.

Per serving: calories 190; fat 1g; protein 10g; carbs 38g; fiber 3g.

PISTACHIO AND ORANGE FILO PARCELS

INGREDIENTS

8 sheets of filo dough, cut into

6-inch squares

1 cup pistachios, finely crushed

Zest of 1 orange

1/4 cup sugar

1/2 cup melted butter

Powdered sugar for dusting

DIRECTIONS

- Mix pistachios, orange zest, and sugar in a bowl.
- Brush a filo square with melted butter, place another square on top, and brush again. Place about 2 Tbsp of pistachio mixture in the center.
- Fold edges over to form a parcel, sealing with butter.
- Air fry at 360°F for about 8 mins or until golden.
- Dust with powdered sugar before serving.

Per serving: calories 360; fat 22g; protein 6g; carbs 34g; fiber 3g.

AIR-FRIED APPLE CHIPS

INGREDIENTS

2 large apples, thinly sliced

1 tsp cinnamon

DIRECTIONS

- Toss apple slices with cinnamon until evenly coated.
- Arrange slices in a single layer in the air fryer basket.
- Air fry at 320°F for about 15 minutes, flipping halfway through, until crisp.

Per serving: calories 50; fat 0g; protein 0g; carbs 13g; fiber 2g.

DATE AND WALNUT STUFFED PEARS

SERVES 4 | PREP 15 MIN | COOK 10 MIN

INGREDIENTS

4 ripe pears, halved and cored

1/2 cup dates, chopped

1/2 cup walnuts, chopped

1 tsp cinnamon

1/4 tsp nutmeg

Optional: drizzle of honey or maple syrup for extra

DIRECTIONS

- Combine dates, walnuts, cinnamon, and nutmeg in a bowl.
- Stuff the pear halves with the date and walnut mixture.
- Air fry at 360°F for about 10 mins or until the pears are tender.
- Drizzle with honey or maple syrup if desired.

Per serving: calories 210; fat 8g; protein 2g; carbs 35g; fiber 5g

GREEK YOGURT CHEESECAKE WITH BERRY COMPOTE

SERVES 4 | PREP 20 MIN | COOK 30 MIN

INGREDIENTS

- **For the cheesecake:**
  - 2 cups Greek yogurt
  - 1/2 cup sugar
  - 2 large eggs
  - 2 Tbsp all-purpose flour
  - 1 tsp vanilla extract
  - Zest of 1 lemon

- **For the berry compote:**
  - 2 cups mixed berries (such as strawberries, blueberries, raspberries)
  - 1/4 cup sugar
  - 1 tsp lemon juice

DIRECTIONS

- **For the cheesecake:**
  - Mix Greek yogurt, sugar, eggs, flour, vanilla extract, and lemon zest until smooth.
  - Pour into a greased springform pan that fits your air fryer.
  - Air fry at 300°F for about 25-30 minutes or until set.
  - Let cool and then chill in the refrigerator for at least 2 hours.

- **For the berry compote:**
  - Combine berries, sugar, and lemon juice in a saucepan over medium heat.
  - Cook until berries break down and sauce thickens about 10 minutes.
  - Let cool slightly before serving over the cheesecake.

Per serving: calories 320; fat 8g; protein 10g; carbs 50g; fiber 2g.

AIR-FRIED BANANA WITH HONEY AND NUTS

INGREDIENTS

4 ripe bananas, peeled and sliced lengthwise

2 Tbsp honey

1/4 cup chopped nuts (such as walnuts, pecans, or almonds)

DIRECTIONS

- Place banana slices in the air fryer basket.
- Air fry at 360°F for about 8 mins or until golden and slightly caramelized.
- Drizzle with honey and sprinkle with chopped nuts before serving.

Per serving: calories 180; fat 5g; protein 2g; carbs 35g; fiber 3g

RICOTTA AND LEMON ZEST FRITTERS

INGREDIENTS

1 cup ricotta cheese

Zest of 1 lemon

1/4 cup all-purpose flour

1 egg

2 Tbsp sugar

1/2 tsp vanilla extract

Powdered sugar for dusting

DIRECTIONS

- In a bowl, mix ricotta, lemon zest, flour, egg, sugar, and vanilla until well combined.
- Form the mixture into small balls.
- Air fry at 360°F for about 10 mins or until golden and slightly crispy.
- Dust with powdered sugar before serving.

Per serving: calories 200; fat 8g; protein 9g; carbs 20g; fiber 0g

CHOCOLATE AND ALMOND STUFFED FIGS

INGREDIENTS

8 fresh figs

8 small pieces of dark
chocolate

8 almonds

Optional: Honey or powdered
sugar for drizzling or dusting

DIRECTIONS

- Make a small cut in the bottom of each fig and gently create a pocket inside.
- Insert a piece of chocolate and an almond into each fig.
- Place the stuffed figs in the air fryer basket.
- Air fry at 360°F for about 5 mins, or until the figs are warm and the chocolate has melted.
- Drizzle with honey or dust with powdered sugar before serving, if desired.

Per serving: calories 150; fat 5g; protein 2g; carbs 25g; fiber 3g.

SESAME HONEY TWISTS

SERVES 4 | PREP 15 MIN | COOK 10 MIN

INGREDIENTS

1 cup all-purpose flour

1/4 cup water

1 Tbsp olive oil

1/4 tsp salt

1/2 cup sesame seeds

1/4 cup honey

DIRECTIONS

- In a bowl, mix flour, water, olive oil, and salt to form a smooth dough.
- Divide the dough into small portions and roll each into a long strip.
- Twist each strip and press gently into sesame seeds to coat.
- Drizzle or brush each twist with honey.
- Air fry at 350°F for about 10 mins, turning halfway through, until golden and crispy.

Per serving: calories 280; fat 14g; protein 5g; carbs 35g; fiber 3g.

APRICOT AND PISTACHIO TARTLETS

INGREDIENTS

4 small pre-made tart shells

1/2 cup apricot jam

1/4 cup pistachios, crushed

Optional: Powdered sugar for dusting

DIRECTIONS

- Spoon apricot jam into each tart shell, filling them about three-quarters full.
- Sprinkle crushed pistachios over the jam.
- Place tartlets in the air fryer basket.
- Air fry at 350°F for about 8 minutes, or until the tart shells are golden and the filling is bubbly.
- Dust with powdered sugar before serving, if desired.

Per serving: calories 210; fat 9g; protein 3g; carbs 30g; fiber 1g.

SPICED ORANGE SLICES

INGREDIENTS

3 large oranges, sliced into rounds

1 tsp cinnamon

1/4 tsp nutmeg

Optional: A drizzle of honey or a sprinkle of brown sugar for extra sweetness

DIRECTIONS

- Arrange orange slices in a single layer in the air fryer basket.
- Sprinkle evenly with cinnamon and nutmeg.
- Air fry at 350°F for about 10 minutes, or until the oranges are heated through and slightly caramelized.
- If desired, drizzle with honey or sprinkle with brown sugar before serving.

Per serving: calories 60; fat 0g; protein 1g; carbs 15g; fiber 3g.

LEMON AND LAVENDER CAKES

SERVES 4 | PREP 20 MIN | COOK 10 MIN

INGREDIENTS

For the cakes:

1 cup all-purpose flour

1/2 cup granulated sugar

1/2 tsp baking powder

1/4 tsp salt

1 Tbsp dried lavender, finely chopped or ground

Zest of 1 lemon

1/4 cup unsalted butter, melted

1 large egg

1/2 cup milk

1 tsp vanilla extract

For the glaze:

1/2 cup powdered sugar

1-2 Tbsp lemon juice

DIRECTIONS

- Whisk flour, sugar, baking powder, salt, lavender, and lemon zest in a bowl.
- In another bowl, mix melted butter, egg, milk, and vanilla.
- Combine wet and dry ingredients until smooth.
- Pour into greased muffin cups or cake mold suitable for air frying.
- Air fry at 350°F for 10 minutes, or until done.
- Mix powdered sugar with lemon juice for the glaze; drizzle over cooled cakes.

Per serving: calories 320; fat 12g; protein 4g; carbs 50g; fiber 1g.

PEACH AND RASPBERRY CRISP

SERVES 4 | PREP 10 MIN | COOK 15 MIN

INGREDIENTS

2 cups sliced peaches (fresh or frozen and thawed)

1 cup raspberries (fresh or frozen)

1/2 cup rolled oats

1/4 cup all-purpose flour

1/4 cup brown sugar

1/4 cup cold butter, cubed

1/2 tsp cinnamon

Pinch of salt

DIRECTIONS

- In a bowl, combine peaches and raspberries and distribute evenly into air fryer-safe baking dishes.
- In another bowl, combine oats, flour, brown sugar, cinnamon, and salt. Add butter and rub into the oat mixture using your fingers until crumbly.
- Sprinkle the oat mixture over the fruit.
- Air fry at 350°F for about 15 minutes, or until the topping is golden and the fruit mixture is bubbly.
- Serve warm, optionally, with a scoop of vanilla ice cream.

Per serving: calories 290; fat 12g; protein 3g; carbs 44g; fiber 5g.

AIR-FRIED
SFOGLIATELLE

SERVES 4 | PREP 30 MIN | COOK 10 MIN

INGREDIENTS

For the dough:

1 roll of store-bought puff pastry, thawed

For the filling:

1 cup ricotta cheese, drained

1/4 cup granulated sugar

1 small egg, beaten

Zest of 1 orange

Zest of 1 lemon

1/4 cup semolina or fine cornmeal

1/2 tsp vanilla extract

Pinch of cinnamon

For dusting:

Powdered sugar

DIRECTIONS

1. **Prepare the filling:**
   - In a bowl, mix ricotta, sugar, egg, orange zest, lemon zest, semolina, vanilla extract, and cinnamon until smooth. Set aside.

2. **Prepare the pastry:**
   - Roll out the puff pastry into a long, thin rectangle. Cut into 4-inch-wide strips.
   - Spread a thin layer of the ricotta mixture along the center of each strip.
   - Fold the dough over the filling and roll each strip loosely to form a shell shape, ensuring the layers can expand.

3. **Air-fry the pastry:**
   - Preheat the air fryer to 350°F.
   - Brush the sfogliatelle lightly with a bit of water to prevent drying and place them in the air fryer basket without overcrowding.
   - Air fry for about 10 minutes or until golden brown and crisp.

4. **Serve:**
   - Let cool slightly and dust with powdered sugar before serving.

Per serving: Estimated calories 350; fat 18g; protein 9g; carbs 40g; fiber 2g.

Conclusion

Dear Reader,

As we near the end of this delightful journey through Mediterranean flavors and air fryer mastery, I wanted to take a moment to share a more personal note with you. This cookbook is a culmination of my passion for cooking, and each recipe and tip in it carries a part of my heart. Creating this cookbook has been a challenge, but also a joy, as I am committed to sharing healthy and efficient meals with you.

I hope that these 150 quick and easy recipes have not only introduced new flavors to your table but have also inspired a healthier way of living. Every meal is an opportunity to nourish both body and soul, and to savor the vibrant colors anDiscd robust flavors that define Mediterranean cuisine.

Your feedback is incredibly valuable to me. If you've enjoyed the flavors and found the recipes beneficial, please consider leaving a review. Sharing your experiences can inspire others to embark on their own journey of health and taste and help us grow and improve together. Your thoughts and insights enrich our community and contribute to the ongoing celebration of healthy, joyful eating.

Thank you from the bottom of my heart for inviting me into your kitchen and for every moment you've dedicated to exploring these pages. Together, we've done more than share recipes; we've nurtured a community passionate about good food and a healthy lifestyle.

With gratitude,
James Marcelli, your culinary companion

30-Day Meal Plan

Day	Appetizer	Lunch	Dinner	Dessert
1	Air-fried falafel	Pistachio crusted salmon	Mediterranean herb chicken	Air-fried baklava bites
2	Bruschetta with tomato and basil	Mediterranean tuna patties	Greek turkey meatballs	Fig and honey yogurt cups
3	Spanakopita triangles	Lemon dill salmon	Shawarma-style chicken	Pistachio and orange filo parcels
4	Crispy artichoke hearts	Garlic butter shrimp	Turkish chicken kebabs	Air-fried apple chips
5	Mediterranean stuffed peppers	Crispy air fried calamari	Chicken parmesan	Date and walnut stuffed pears
6	Zucchini chips	Mediterranean salmon steak	Lemon garlic turkey breasts	Greek yogurt cheesecake with berry compote
7	Kale chips	Sea bass with Mediterranean spice rub	Chicken and artichoke hearts	Air-fried banana with honey and nuts
8	Feta cheese bites	Cajun shrimp	Spiced turkey patties	Ricotta and lemon zest fritters
9	Air-fried olives	Air-fried scallops with lemon butter sauce	Chicken souvlaki	Chocolate and almond stuffed figs
10	Baba ghanoush with air-fried veggie chips	Sweet chili shrimp	Paprika and lime chicken drumsticks	Sesame honey twists
11	Garlic shrimps	Spiced cod with chickpeas	Mediterranean stuffed chicken	Apricot and pistachio tartlets
12	Mozzarella sticks	Pesto shrimp with zucchini noodles	Crispy Dijon chicken	Spiced orange slices
13	Greek meatballs	Herb fish cakes	Turkey and spinach pinwheels	Lemon and lavender cakes
14	Crispy cauliflower with tahini sauce	Tilapia with caper lemon butter	Turkey and vegetable skewers	Peach and raspberry crisp
15	Eggplant rollatini	Halibut with garlic lemon aioli	Chicken and olive tagine	Air-fried sfogliatelle

Day	Appetizer	Lunch	Dinner	Dessert
16	Mushroom caps with herb cheese	Tilapia with olive tapenade	Garlic and herb turkey tenderloin	Fig and honey yogurt cups
17	Air-fried cod cakes	Beef kofta kebabs	Chicken caprese	Date and walnut stuffed pears
18	Lemon herb scallops	Mediterranean beef patties	Greek chicken pitas	Pistachio and orange filo parcels
19	Air-fried falafel	Stuffed bell peppers	Beef and feta stuffed zucchini	Air-fried apple chips
20	Crispy artichoke hearts	Shawarma-style beef	Smoky espresso steak	Greek yogurt cheesecake with berry compote
21	Zucchini chips	Beef souvlaki	Beef and olive empanadas	Air-fried banana with honey and nuts
22	Kale chips	Greek lamb meatballs	Lamb chops with rosemary	Ricotta and lemon zest fritters
23	Feta cheese bites	Air-fried lamb gyros	Lamb and pine nut mini pies	Chocolate and almond stuffed figs
24	Air-fried olives	Lamb stuffed eggplant	Lamb fajitas	Sesame honey twists
25	Baba ghanoush with air-fried veggie chips	Spiced lamb ribs	Greek-style pork chops	Apricot and pistachio tartlets
26	Garlic shrimps	Italian herb pork tenderloin	Smoky paprika pork kebabs	Spiced orange slices
27	Mozzarella sticks	Crispy chickpea falafel	Stuffed tomatoes	Lemon and lavender cakes
28	Greek meatballs	Artichoke and spinach dip	Air-fried dolmas	Peach and raspberry crisp
29	Bruschetta with tomato and basil	Pistachio crusted salmon	Chicken parmesan	Spiced orange slices
30	Mediterranean stuffed peppers	Garlic butter shrimp	Chicken caprese	Air-fried baklava bites

Air Fryer Conversion Chart

Conventional Oven (°C)	Air Fryer (°C)
120°C (250°F)	100°C (212°F)
150°C (300°F)	130°C (266°F)
160°C (325°F)	140°C (284°F)
180°C (350°F)	160°C (320°F)
190°C (375°F)	170°C (338°F)
200°C (400°F)	180°C (356°F)
220°C (425°F)	200°C (392°F)
230°C (450°F)	210°C (410°F)
240°C (475°F)	220°C (428°F)

Conversion Chart

Volume Equivalents (Liquid)

US Customary Quantity	Metric Equivalent
1 teaspoon	5 mL
1 tablespoon	15 mL
2 tablespoons	30 mL
1/4 cup or 2 fluid ounces	60 mL
1/3 cup	80 mL
1/2 cup or 4 fluid ounces	125 mL
2/3 cup	160 mL
3/4 cup or 6 fluid ounces	180 mL
1 cup or 8 fluid ounces or 1/2 pint	250 mL
1 ½ cup or 12 fluid ounces	375 mL
2 cups or 1 pint or 16 fluid ounces	500 mL
3 cups or 1 ½ pints	700 mL
4 cups or 2 pints or 1 quart	950 mL
4 quarts or 1 gallon	3.8 L
1 ounce	28 grams
1/4 lb. (4 ounces)	112 grams
1/2 lb. (8 ounces)	225 grams
3/4 lb. (12 ounces)	337 grams
1 lb. (16 ounces)	450 grams

Volume Equivalents (Dry)

US Customary Quantity	Metric Equivalent
1 ounce	28 grams
4 ounces or 1/4 lb.	113 grams
1/3 lb.	150 grams
8 ounces or ½ lb.	230 grams
2/3 lb.	300 grams
12 ounces or ¾ lb.	340 grams
16 ounces or 1 lb.	450 grams
32 ounces or 2 lbs.	900 grams